CREATIVE MICROWAVE COOKING

Irena Chalmers
Richard Ahrens and Ruth Malinowski

WEATHERVANE
BOOKS

PICTURE CREDITS

The following pictures were provided through the
courtesy of Transworld Feature Syndicate, Inc.:

Syndication International: pp. 11   17   19   21   25
27   29   34   38 & 39   43   45   46   47   49   51   52
54   56 & 57   58 & 59   62 & 63   66 & 67   68 & 69   70
80   89   93   94   96   111   121   128   131   135   138
139   142

Lennart Osbeck: pp. 31   77   85   107   109   125   133
Scoop: pp. 75   91   100   114
Michael Holtz: pp. 53   73   101
Euphot: pp. 112 & 113
Studio Conti: p. 23

Contents

preface

The microwave oven has recently moved from the heady realms of luxury into the area of practical necessity. It is now possible to prepare a meal in only a fraction of the time needed to cook by more traditional methods. The manufacturers have improved the performance of the oven to the point that it is not only conceivable but very likely that it may soon supplement or replace the conventional range completely. Already microwave ovens are seen as an essential appliance for every modern kitchen.

The microwave oven eliminates the necessity to plan meals ahead. Even long-cooking foods are ready in minutes rather than hours. Foods can be taken directly from the freezer and defrosted in a very short period of time. With a well-stocked freezer there is always something good to eat both for the family and for unexpected guests. Late arrivals can have a plate of appetizing hot food ready to eat in seconds. The meal will have all the qualities of freshly cooked food, for one of the great advantages of cooking in the microwave oven is that reheated food does not become dry, as is often the case with foods reheated in the conventional oven or on top of the range. Instead the colors remain bright and clear, the food is moist and tasty, and more of the nutrients are retained because the cooking time is so brief.

The microwave oven uses less energy to cook food than does the conventional oven. The microwave oven does not need to be preheated, but instead the cooking starts the moment the door is closed. There are few spills, and the oven needs only a quick flip of a sponge to become spotlessly clean. As all the cooking is done in glass, china, or ceramic utensils or with paper products, the clean-up chores are finished very quickly.

The oven is useful not only for the preparation of entire meals but for speeding separate steps in the cooking; for melting butter and chocolate, for heating liquids, for drying bread crumbs, for toasting nuts, and for a thousand other time-consuming processes.

Having a microwave oven in the kitchen is like having two extra pairs of hands working for you, and, though nothing makes cooking entirely effortless, the microwave oven makes everything faster and easier.

introduction

How Does It Work?

Imagine you are walking beside a still, quiet pond. It is a windless day and the surface of the water is calm and smooth. If you throw a stone into the pond, it will sink, and ripples or waves will be produced in ever-widening circles radiating from the point at which the stone entered the water. The circles of waves that are generated will be of different sizes; the inner, shorter waves will travel faster and with greater energy than the outer waves.

Electromagnetic waves are short waves that travel at the speed of light, 186,000 miles per second. These waves carry photons that vibrate to produce energy. The number or frequency of the vibrations determines the amount of energy produced.

In a microwave oven the microwaves are produced by a magnetron. This is the equivalent of throwing a stone in a pond. The microwaves are produced the moment the oven door is closed by the conversion of electricity to electromagnetic energy. When the microwaves enter the oven, they are interrupted by a stirrer that scatters and distributes them evenly throughout the interior of the oven. The microwaves then enter the food, and the vibration of the waves produces heat energy that is absorbed from the outside to the center of the food. It is the intramolecular friction that produces the heat to cook the food. The higher the moisture content of the food, the faster it will cook. Microwaves cause the moisture cells within the food to vibrate at approximately two and a half million times a second. This is why microwave cooking is so much faster than conventional conduction cooking.

Understanding The Microwave Oven

If you heat a cup of water in a saucepan on top of the stove, it will reach the boiling point more rapidly over high heat than if you put it on a low flame.

If you heat a cup of water in the microwave oven, it will take roughly 2 minutes to reach the boiling point. There is no equivalent of a high flame in the microwave oven. It takes all the available microwave energy to make this quantity of water boil. Therefore, if it takes 2 minutes for 1 cup of water to boil, it will take more energy,—that is, more time—for 2 cups of water to reach the boiling point.

If you put a cup of hot water in the microwave oven, it will reach the boiling point more rapidly than a cup of iced water. If you defrost food taken from a freezer at 0 degrees, it will take longer to defrost than food from the freezer above the refrigerator. A refrigerator freezer cannot maintain as low a temperature as a separate freezer.

If you bake 1 potato in the conventional oven at 350° F, it will take 1 hour to cook. It will take the same length of time if you bake 2 or 6 potatoes simultaneously. This is because all the potatoes are equally surrounded by a mass of hot air. If you lower the temperature, the potatoes will take longer to cook. If you increase the temperature, they will cook more rapidly.

However, if you put 1 potato in the microwave oven, it will be baked in 4 minutes. All the available microwave energy is used in cooking the single potato. The air in the microwave oven remains at room temperature. It therefore takes a longer time to cook 2 or more potatoes.

If you reheat bread, it will be hot faster than if you reheat a pork chop. Bread is more porous than meat.

If you cook an unevenly shaped food, such as a leg of lamb, in the microwave oven, it will cook in the same way as in the conventional oven to the extent that the thinner parts will cook more quickly than the thicker parts. To cook food evenly, thinner parts can be protected by wrapping them in lightweight aluminum foil halfway through the cooking period.

Although the "heat" cannot be increased in the microwave oven, the amount of energy reaching the food can be decreased. Every oven manufacturer uses different but similar terminology in differentiating between the highest setting, roast and simmer settings and the slower speed of the defrost setting, but they all follow the same patterns. Do be sure to read the written material that accompanies every new microwave oven, because, in order to get the maximum satisfaction from the oven, you must understand the way it works.

Though all these facts are obvious, and I hesitate to mention them, they are, surprisingly, not nearly as apparent when you first start cooking with microwave energy. You may at first be quite impatient with the oven, but after a very short time and with the help of a little experience you will soon not only become used to it but quite dependent on it, too. At this point you will be able to adapt your favorite recipes for the oven and save hours of cooking time.

Assessing the Microwave Oven

All scientific, industrial, medical, and cooking equipment that uses shortwave energy is permitted to operate only if it conforms with the strict and rigidly enforced standards of safety established by the Federal Communications Commission. In spite of rumors to the contrary a microwave oven that is not in use is no more hazardous than a television set or a radio that is turned off. Both television sets and radios are powered by microwave energy. There is, furthermore, no possibility of leakage of microwaves when the oven is in actual use. This is because every microwave oven is equipped with a fail-safe mechanism that automatically causes the oven to shut itself off if any part is not functioning correctly.

The unreasoning fear of cooking in a microwave oven has, in the past, been a significant factor in the slow public acceptance of this method of preparing food. Yet this attitude is based on emotion rather than fact. Dread warnings have almost always circulated around new inventions (if man had been meant to fly, he would have been given wings, etc.). Throughout history the stalwart defenders of the status quo have denounced everything from the electric light bulb to the automobile, but the time interval between the proposal of a new idea and its acceptance by the mass market is becoming shorter and shorter, and it will not be many years before the microwave oven is a standard part of every new kitchen.

Why Metal Must Not Be Used in the Microwave Oven

The walls of the microwave oven are made of metal. Metal reflects microwaves like a mirror to bounce the energy into the cavity of the oven. If a metal pan or any other metal object is placed in the oven, the energy bounces off the oven walls to the object, back to the walls, and back again to the object. This causes an effect known as "arcing" and is immediately and dramatically apparent in the form of a series of intensely bright light flashes. This arcing effect will continue until the oven is turned off.

Objects as small as a metal skewer, a meat thermometer, or even the presence of metal in the painted designs on plates will cause arcing. It not only slows down or prevents the cooking of the food, but it can also cause serious and irreversible damage to the magnetron that converts electricity to microwave energy.

A lightweight piece of aluminum foil does not cause arcing as long as the foil is not actually touching the walls of the oven, but the heavier weight of a ¾-inch-deep aluminum tray, containing, for example, a TV dinner, cannot be used. The food must be transferred to a plate. If you are in any doubt about a utensil, fill it with a cup of water. If the utensil becomes hot within 2 minutes, do not use it.

Cooking Utensils for the Microwave Oven

Microwaves pass unhindered through glass, ceramics, china, and certain other materials as though they were not there, in a similar way to sunlight passing unobstructed through a window. The sun heats the room while the window remains at the same temperature as the air surrounding it. This is why utensils used in the microwave oven remain cool to the touch even when the food is boiling hot, though sometimes there can be transference of heat from the food to the cooking utensil after a long cooking time.

Glass, ceramics, china, paper, and some plastics can all be used in the oven, both for cooking and for reheating the food. Wax-treated paper can be used, but transparent wraps may melt in the microwave oven.

Pottery and earthenware bowls are suitable for use in the oven if they do not contain any traces of lead or other metal. Clay pots can also be used.

Frozen vegetables can be reheated in their cardboard boxes if one end is opened to allow the steam to escape.

Plastic cooking pouches can be used, but cut a slit in the pouch to allow the steam to escape. Duck can be defrosted in its plastic wrapping, but again be sure to cut a slit for steam to escape.

"Take out" foods can be reheated in the carrying containers unless the boxes are sealed with metal staples.

Advantages of Cooking in a Microwave Oven

SPEED

A simple meal for one or two people can be prepared in one-quarter to one-fifth of the conventional cooking time. (Larger quantities of food require longer cooking times.)

CONVENIENCE

Frozen foods can be defrosted in a fraction of the conventional time. Foods prepared in advance need only seconds to reheat and look and taste as appetizing as when they were first made.

CLEAN COOKING

The oven is very quick and easily cleaned. The cooking utensils can all be put into a dishwasher, and paper products used for cooking are thrown away.

COOL COOKING

The kitchen does not become hot because the food is cooked by internal friction and the heat remains confined to the food itself.

BABY FOODS

Baby foods and bottles can be warmed in their own containers, with the metal lids removed. A jar of junior food is warmed in 30 seconds.

Quick-Cooking Techniques

The total length of time spent in the preparation of many foods can be considerably reduced by the use of the microwave oven. The oven is used on the highest setting for all the following preparations.

To soften butter, place the butter in a small bowl—2 tablespoons of butter are softened in 15 seconds; 2 tablespoons of butter are sizzling hot in 40 seconds.

To melt chocolate, put it on a plate and soften 6 ounces of semisweet chocolate pieces in 1 minute, without added water.

To toast nuts and bread crumbs, spread them on a plate and cook a 1-cup quantity for 3 minutes, stirring every minute.

To heat maple syrup for pancakes, remove the lid from the container and cook for 30 seconds. (Sugar heats very quickly in the microwave oven.)

To speed the defrosting of frozen juices, remove the metal cap from the container and heat for 1 minute. (The metal base will not cause the arcing effect usually seen when metal is used in the microwave oven.)

To prepare hot drinks, fill a cup with the liquid and heat for 2 minutes.

To peel tomatoes, peaches, and other soft foods, heat them for 30 seconds and let stand for 2 minutes. If the fruit is underripe, heat for 10 seconds longer.

To obtain more juice from lemons and other citrus fruits, heat for 30 seconds. This technique can also be used before processing vegetable juices in a juice extractor.

To soften dried fruits, place 1 cup of raisins, prunes, apples, or apricots in a bowl. Cover with water and heat for 5 minutes.

To caramelize sugar for making caramel custard or butterscotch sauce, place ½ cup sugar in a bowl and cook for 3 minutes, until a golden brown liquid is formed.

To speed the preparation time of foods cooked on an outdoor grill, precook the food for half the estimated cooking time in the microwave oven. Finish the cooking on the grill outside. Precooking prevents the outside of the food from becoming charred while the inside is still raw.

To heat a sandwich filling, place it on a plate, making a depression in the center. Heat for 1 minute. Microwaves are attracted to the edges of the food rather than the center. Toast or heat buns or breads separately.

To dry herbs, spread paper towels on paper plates, put the herbs on the paper towels, and heat for 50 seconds. Allow to stand for 10 seconds and repeat for 10-second cooking-time intervals until completely dry. Discard stems and place herbs in clean, dry jars with tightly fitting lids. Store in a dark place.

To melt preserves for glazes and the foundations of dessert sauces, heat them in the jar, with the lid removed, for 5 minutes; then strain the preserves.

Disadvantages of Cooking in a Microwave Oven

ACCURATE TIMING

Microwave ovens vary in efficiency, and it is therefore important to refer to the literature that accompanies your own model. Other variations in cooking times will result from the quality of the ingredients, the starting temperature, and the shape of the food. It is as necessary to use your own judgment in assessing when the food is ready as it is in cooking by conventional means.

Remember that the food cooked in a microwave oven will continue to cook after it is removed from the oven for times ranging from a few seconds to several minutes, depending on the density of the food. It is as easy to overcook as it is to undercook foods and, as with all things, experience is the only reliable guide to absolute perfection.

TEXTURE

It is thought by some people that the texture of meat is changed and softened when cooked in the microwave oven. This is a question of personal taste, and an individual judgment must be made on the question of whether a slight alteration is justified by the greatly increased speed in cooking.

Great care must be taken in reheating bread and pastry, as the texture becomes rapidly softened.

Foods enclosed in a skin or membrane, such as potatoes, kidneys, liver, oysters, escargots, and eggs tend to "explode" in the microwave oven. There are those who claim that these foods can be cooked triumphantly with microwave energy, but I have not met with similar success in spite of repeated attempts to duplicate their cleverness. I have found that this group of foods is much better cooked by conventional means. See specific recipes for further information.

Foods do not achieve a brown, crisp crust when cooked in the microwave oven. This effect can be achieved only in the conventional oven.

All foods cook more rapidly at the edges than in the center. Soft and semisoft foods must be stirred, and solid foods must be rotated to compensate for this effect.

No metal utensils can be used in the microwave oven.

Food for a complete meal must be cooked in a sequence rather than simultaneously; that is, the meat is cooked first, then the starch (potatoes or rice), and finally the vegetables. The greater the overall volume of food in the microwave oven, the slower the cooking process.

Salt

Do not sprinkle the surface of meats with salt before cooking, as salt distorts the pattern of the microwaves and makes a tough exterior. However, salt can be added to foods cooked in a liquid. Where exceptions to this rule occur, they have been noted in specific recipes.

Covering the Pans

When a recipe calls for the ingredients to be covered, a nonmetallic lid should be used: a glass or ceramic casserole top, a plate, or a piece of waxed paper. The main purpose of covering the food is to prevent splattering in the oven. While some foods are covered to prevent them from becoming dry, the drying-out of food is less of a problem in microwave cooking than in the conventional oven, because the air surrounding the food in the microwave oven is cold and moist. In the conventional oven it is hot and dry.

Time Settings in the Microwave Oven

The recipes in this book are all cooked on the highest setting unless otherwise stated. The highest setting allows the maximum energy to cook the food. When the setting is reduced to "roast," "defrost," or other speeds, part of the microwaves are prevented from entering the oven by an "on-off" system. In the "defrost" setting, for example, the oven is in effect on for eight-tenths of a second and off for two-tenths of a second. (Different ovens vary in the "on-off" cycles.) By controlling the amount of energy, the rate of cooking is also controlled.

In passing, it is interesting to note that the highest setting is used less frequently than the lower settings. There is a great improvement in the quality of the food if it is cooked at a slightly lower speed than the maximum available.

appetizers

swiss fondue

swiss fondue

Though either Swiss or Gruyère can be used for making fondue, the imported cheese from the mountainous Gruyère region of Switzerland gives the deepest, creamiest, and richest flavor.

Yield: 8 servings

1 cup white wine
  (Chablis or California white wine)
2 whole cloves garlic, peeled
¾ pound (3 cups) grated Gruyère or
  Swiss cheese
3 tablespoons flour

Freshly ground black pepper
3 tablespoons kirsch
3 tablespoons butter
¼ cup heavy cream
1 teaspoon salt

Pour the wine into a 1½-quart earthenware pot, a clay pot, or a glass casserole. Add the garlic. Cook uncovered on "simmer" setting for 5 minutes. Discard the garlic cloves.

Combine the cheese, flour, and pepper and stir into the hot wine. Simmer for 3 minutes. Stir in the kirsch, butter, and cream. Simmer for 4 more minutes. Season with salt.

Serve immediately with cubes of fresh, crusty French bread and chilled white wine. Spear the bread cubes with fondue forks and swirl into the hot fondue.

Mushroom caps, quickly fried in hot butter, as well as salami, carrot sticks, and cauliflower sprigs, make delicious contrasts of taste and texture with the fondue. In Switzerland there is also a bowl of pickled onions and potatoes boiled in their jackets to eat with the fondue.

marinated steak kebabs

These appetizers are marinated in wine, cooked at the last moment, and served sizzling hot, tender, and juicy.

Yield: 6 servings

1 pound sirloin steak, weighed without the bone
½ cup red wine
2 tablespoons oil
1 tablespoon soy sauce
1 clove garlic, finely chopped
2 tablespoons cracked black pepper
2 tablespoons oil

Cut the steak into bite-size cubes and place in a bowl. Add the wine, 2 tablespoons oil, soy sauce, and garlic. Marinate the steak for 2 hours. Remove and dry on paper towels. Press the cracked pepper onto the surface of the beef.

Heat the ceramic browning plate on the highest setting for 4 minutes. Add the remaining 2 tablespoons oil. Add the steak cubes and cook for 2 minutes on each side. They should be rare in the center. Serve with toothpicks.

Note: A ceramic browning plate is supplied with some models of microwave ovens. If your oven does not have one, use a shallow Corning ™ skillet.

paté maison

This paté is as good as any you will eat anywhere. Serve on freshly made toast with cocktails or for a first course. French cornichons or small gherkins and tiny onions browned in butter are good accompaniments.

Yield: 10 servings

½ pound ground raw pork
1 pound ground raw veal
1 pound ground raw calves liver
2 cloves garlic, finely chopped
¾ teaspoon thyme
¼ teaspoon nutmeg
1 teaspoon salt

Freshly ground black pepper
2 tablespoons brandy
2 tablespoons Madeira
½ cup heavy cream
2 eggs, lightly beaten
4 chicken livers, cut in half
6 slices bacon

Combine all ingredients except the chicken livers and bacon in a large bowl. Do not stir too much or the mixture becomes heavy.

Place half of the mixture in a 9 x 5 x 2½-inch glass loaf pan. Arrange the chicken livers in a row down the length of the pan and cover with the remaining mixture. Arrange the bacon in overlapping slices on top of the paté.

Cook on "roast" setting for 25 minutes. Rotate the pan one-quarter of a turn after 10 minutes.

Cool the paté. Cover with aluminum foil and weight the paté with 3 1-pound cans of food so it can be sliced without crumbling. Chill for 48 hours before serving.

scallops in lime juice

The success of this almost-instant appetizer is entirely dependent on the freshness of the scallops. Naturally tender enough to be eaten raw, when scallops are cooked briefly, they absorb the flavor of the other ingredients. They are also superb in a cold mixed-seafood salad.

Yield: 8 servings

1 pound bay scallops*
1 paper-thin slice fresh ginger root, minced
1 teaspoon sugar
Juice of 1 lime
¼ teaspoon salt

Toss all ingredients except the salt together in a shallow glass dish. Cook on the highest setting for 2 minutes. Stir once so that the scallops cook evenly. Season with salt.

The scallops can be served immediately or chilled for 4 hours and served with small pieces of avocado, pimiento, or chopped tomato. A few pitted green and black olives make an attractive garnish.

*Sea scallops may also be used; cut them into smaller pieces.

coquilles st. jacques

This elegant appetizer is ready in only a fraction of the conventional cooking time.

Yield: 4 servings

1 pound bay scallops*
¼ cup white vermouth
1 cup water
¼ teaspoon tarragon
2 tablespoons finely chopped parsley
2 tablespoons butter
4 mushrooms, thinly sliced
2 tablespoons flour
2 egg yolks
¼ cup heavy cream
4 tablespoons freshly grated Parmesan cheese
2 tablespoons butter

Place the scallops, vermouth, water, tarragon and parsley in a small glass or ceramic casserole. Cover and cook on the highest setting for 2 minutes. Drain the scallops and reserve the liquid.

Heat 2 tablespoons of butter in a small bowl. Add and cook the mushrooms for 2 minutes. Stir in the flour and the reserved liquid. Stir in the egg yolks and whipping cream. Combine with the scallops and place in scallop shells or ramekins.

When ready to serve, reheat in the microwave oven on "reheat" setting for 2 minutes. Sprinkle with cheese, dot with butter, and place under the preheated broiler of a conventional oven for 3 minutes, until the cheese is lightly browned.

*Sea scallops may also be used; cut them into smaller pieces.

meatball appetizers

Meatballs are cooked so quickly in the microwave oven that they remain moist but will not fall apart. Serve them with toothpicks and dip into mustard.

Yield: 30 1-inch meatballs

1 egg
1 teaspoon soy sauce
Freshly ground black pepper
½ teaspoon thyme
1 tablespoon oil

1 pound ground lean chuck steak
¼ cup fine fresh bread crumbs
½ small onion, finely chopped
1 tablespoon meat sauce such as A-1
¼ cup milk

Place all ingredients except the oil in a bowl and stir lightly with a fork until just combined. Do not overmix or the meatballs will become heavy. Form the mixture into 1-inch balls.

Heat a ceramic plate on the highest setting for 4 minutes. Add the oil. Cook 10 meatballs at a time for 1 minute on each side. Rotate the dish one-quarter of a turn after the first minute.

salted shrimps

Nothing could be simpler, but this appetizer is always a huge success. Give each person a finger bowl of warm water, and float a slice of lemon in each bowl.

Yield: 4 servings

1 pound jumbo shrimps with the shells on
2 tablespoons oil
Kosher or coarse salt

Rinse and dry the shrimps on paper towels. Heat the oil on a ceramic plate for 1 minute on the highest setting. Spread the shrimps on the plate and cook for 3 minutes on the same setting, until the shells are bright pink. Stir and turn the shrimps once to be sure all are cooked evenly. Immediately roll the shrimps in salt and serve hot.

garlic shrimps

This is a Spanish recipe and very good to serve with drinks before dinner. Use large, fresh shrimps.

Yield: 4 servings

1½ pounds shrimps, peeled and deveined
4 cloves garlic, peeled and left whole
4 tablespoons olive oil
1 tablespoon lemon juice
½ teaspoon tarragon

Place the shrimps in a shallow glass or ceramic baking dish with all the remaining ingredients.

Cook 8 minutes on highest setting, until shrimps are pink. Turn the shrimps and rotate the dish one quarter of a turn after 4 minutes. Serve hot, using toothpicks to pick up the shrimps.

shrimps with tarragon

The marvelous flavor of the shrimps is every bit as good as the exquisite aroma.

Yield: 6 servings

1 pound jumbo shrimps, shelled, but with the tails left on
1 tablespoon oil
2 tablespoons chopped scallions
1 clove garlic, finely chopped
½ teaspoon tarragon
½ cup white vermouth
Salt and pepper

Devein the shrimps and cut lengthwise in half, keeping the tail attached.

Heat a ceramic plate on highest setting for 4 minutes. Add the oil, scallions, garlic, tarragon, and white vermouth and cook for 1 minute. Add the shrimps and continue cooking for 3 minutes. Turn the shrimps once and rotate the dish one-quarter of a turn to ensure that all the shrimps are cooked evenly. Serve hot, seasoned with salt and pepper.

stuffed vine leaves

This is a favorite Greek recipe that is very successfully cooked in the microwave oven.

Yield: 6 servings

1 jar (16 ounces) vine leaves
1½ tablespoons olive oil
1 medium-size onion, finely chopped
¾ cup rice
1½ cups water
½ cup white raisins soaked in ½ cup water
½ cup pine nuts
2 tablespoons finely chopped parsley
½ teaspoon salt
Freshly ground black pepper
½ teaspoon cinnamon
2 medium-size tomatoes, peeled, seeded, and chopped
Water
Juice of 1 lemon

Unfold the vine leaves carefully and rinse under cold running water. Drain. Heat the olive oil in a 1-quart glass or ceramic casserole on the highest setting for 30 seconds. Add the onion and cook 1 minute. Add the rice and cook 2 minutes. Stir in the water, drained raisins, and pine nuts. Cover and cook 10 minutes. Remove and let stand for 10 minutes. Stir in the parsley, salt, pepper, cinnamon, and tomatoes.

Place approximately 1 tablespoon of the mixture on each vine leaf. Fold up the stem end to enclose the stuffing. Fold the sides to the center and roll to form a neat package. The vine leaves will hold together without any other means of securing them.

Place a layer of vine leaves in a glass baking dish. Cover with a layer of unfilled vine leaves and cover with a second layer of stuffed vine leaves. Add sufficient water to barely cover the vine leaves and add the lemon juice. Weight with a plate. Cover with waxed paper and cook for 20 minutes on the highest setting. Allow to cool for 1 hour. Drain and chill until serving time. Serve cold.

rice

Rice is cooked in the microwave oven in 10 minutes. As it can be reheated very successfully, it may be convenient for you to double the recipe and keep a supply of cooked rice in the refrigerator. To reheat, place the rice in a small casserole. Cover and cook for 1 minute.

Yield: 6 servings

2 cups boiling water	**1 tablespoon butter**
½ teaspoon salt	**1 cup long-grain rice**

Pour the water into a 1-quart glass casserole. Add the remaining ingredients. Cover and cook for 10 minutes on the highest setting. Remove from the oven and let stand for 10 more minutes.

Picture on next page: stuffed vine leaves

chicken terrine

A 1½-quart clay or earthenware dish can be used for preparing this dish, or use a deep glass or ceramic casserole. Serve as an appetizer or lunch dish with a salad.

Yield: 8 servings

1 3-pound cooked chicken
1 pound raw pork sausage meat
½ pound sliced boiled ham, diced
2 cloves garlic, finely chopped
2 eggs, lightly beaten
1 teaspoon tarragon

1 tablespoon finely chopped parsley
¼ cup brandy
½ teaspoon salt
Freshly ground black pepper
½ cup butter, softened
½ pound sliced bacon

Discard the skin and bone and cut the chicken into small pieces. Leave to one side. Stir together all remaining ingredients except the bacon.

Line a glass or ceramic casserole with half the bacon slices. Cover with one-third the sausage mixture and top with half the chicken. Continue forming layers, top with the sausage mixture, and cover with the remaining bacon.

Cook in the microwave oven on "roast" setting for 25 minutes. Rotate the dish one-quarter of a turn after 15 minutes. Cool the terrine. Place it in the refrigerator and weight it with 3 1-pound cans of food so it can be sliced without crumbling. Chill 12 hours before serving.

savory butter scones

Scones may be cooked a day ahead and warmed for 2 to 3 minutes on "reheat" setting.

Yield: About 15

2 cups self-rising flour
1 teaspoon baking powder
½ teaspoon salt
2 tablespoons butter
½ cup cheese, grated
1 pimiento (canned)

1 small onion, finely chopped
1 clove garlic, crushed
1 teaspoon chopped parsley
¼ cup milk, approximately
⅓ cup butter, melted

Sift dry ingredients into a bowl and cut in butter with 2 knives or a pastry blender. Add the cheese, chopped pimiento, onion, garlic, and parsley. Mix with enough milk to make a soft but not sticky dough. Line the bottom of an 8-inch glass baking dish with waxed paper. Pat out mixture in dish. Cook on "simmer" setting for 7 minutes and then on highest setting for 3 to 4 minutes. Remove from oven and pour melted butter over the surface. Let stand for 5 minutes to set. Cut into fingers 1½ x 3 inches and serve while hot.

Picture on next page:
(clockwise from top left)

french fruit tarts
savory butter scones
hazelnut cookies

stuffed sausages
chocolate frosted brownies

(center)
chicken patties
anchovy fingers
spinach tarts

vichyssoise

Vichyssoise is the cold summer soup that was created in 1910 by chef Louis Diat to honor the gala opening of the roof garden at the Ritz Carlton Hotel in New York City. The soup was an instant success and is still as popular as it was in the first public unveiling of the masterpiece.

Yield: 6 servings

2 pounds potatoes (about 4 medium-size potatoes)
6 leeks or 3 yellow onions, finely chopped
6 cups chicken broth, hot
1 cup heavy cream
1 teaspoon salt
Chopped chives
Freshly ground black pepper

Peel the potatoes, cut into small pieces, and place in a 2-quart glass or ceramic casserole. Slice the white part and the lower third of the green part of the leeks. Wash in plenty of cold water to remove sand from the leeks. Add the leeks or onions to the potatoes along with the hot chicken broth. Cover and cook on the highest setting for 10 minutes, until the potatoes are very soft. Purée the soup in a blender. Add the cream and salt and chill for 4 hours before serving. Garnish with chopped chives and black pepper.
Note: Cold soups need more salt than hot soups.

watercress and potato soup

If you have never tasted this, you may be surprised to see how such simple ingredients can make such a good soup.

Yield: 4 servings

1 bunch watercress
2 tablespoons butter
1 onion, finely chopped
1 stalk celery, chopped
2 medium-size potatoes, peeled and cut into small pieces
3 cups chicken broth
1 tablespoon lemon juice
½ teaspoon salt
Freshly ground black pepper
½ cup heavy cream

Wash the watercress. Reserve ½ cup of the leaves and chop the remaining leaves and stems into small pieces. Using the highest setting throughout this recipe, heat the butter in a 2-quart glass or ceramic casserole for 20 seconds. Add the onion and celery and cook uncovered for 2 minutes. Add the watercress, potatoes, chicken broth, lemon juice, salt, and pepper. Cover and cook for 15 minutes. Purée these ingredients in the blender and return to the pan. Add the cream and heat for 2 minutes, until very hot. Add the reserved watercress leaves and serve hot or cold.

Picture on next page: watercress and potato soup

tomato soup

Homemade soups are so quickly made in the microwave oven that you can have a different one every day. Tomato soup is at its best in the summer months when the tomatoes are bursting with red, ripe flavor.

Yield: 6 servings

2 pounds Italian plum tomatoes or about 6 medium-size tomatoes
1 onion, chopped
1 stalk celery, chopped
2 cups chicken broth
1 tablespoon tomato paste
1 teaspoon basil or oregano
Freshly ground black pepper
1 teaspoon salt
1 cup yogurt, or sour cream, or heavy cream (optional)

Cut the plum tomatoes in half or cut larger tomatoes into wedges to release the juice. Place in a 3-quart glass or ceramic casserole with the onion and celery. Add the chicken broth, tomato paste, and basil or oregano and season with black pepper.

Cook uncovered on the highest setting for 20 minutes. Season with salt. Strain to remove the tomato skins and seeds. Garnish with spoonfuls of yogurt or sour cream or stir in whipping cream.

crab soup

Crab soup is a glorious, rich, and sumptuous beginning for an elegant meal.

Yield: 6 servings

1½ pounds tomatoes
1 onion, finely chopped
1 cup chicken broth
1 cup clam broth
2 teaspoons tomato paste
2 tablespoons flour
¼ cup Madeira or dry sherry
1 cup heavy cream
½ teaspoon salt
Freshly ground black pepper
1 pound crab meat

Cut the tomatoes into wedges and place in a 2-quart glass or ceramic casserole with the onion. Add the chicken broth, clam broth, and tomato paste. Cook uncovered at the highest setting for 30 minutes. Transfer the soup to a blender and add the flour. Purée the soup until smooth, and strain to remove the tomato skins and seeds. Stir in the Madeira and cream. Season with salt and pepper and heat uncovered for 5 minutes. Add the crab and cook another 5 minutes. Serve hot.

tomato soup

jerusalem artichoke soup

Jerusalem artichokes are native to America, and nobody knows now how they acquired their name. They appear only rarely in supermarkets, but, if you have a garden, they are the most satisfying of vegetables to grow. They are a winter crop, and the more you harvest, the more they appear in underground clusters.

Yield: 6 servings

1 pound Jerusalem artichokes
1 tablespoon lemon juice
3 cups chicken broth
2 tablespoons butter
2 tablespoons flour
1 cup milk
1 cup light cream
1 teaspoon salt
Freshly ground black pepper
½ cup freshly grated Parmesan cheese

Peel the artichokes and place them in a 2-quart glass saucepan. Add the lemon juice and enough water to cover. Cover and cook on the highest setting for 15 minutes, until very tender. Drain the artichokes and place in the blender with 1 cup of chicken broth. Purée until smooth.

Heat the butter on the highest setting for 30 seconds, and stir in the flour. Stir in the remaining chicken broth, artichoke purée, milk, cream, salt, and pepper. Cook uncovered for 6 minutes. Sprinkle with Parmesan cheese at the table.

cream of corn soup

A traditional early American soup that is equally good served hot or cold.

Yield: 4 servings

3 cups chicken broth
1 onion, finely chopped
1 potato, peeled and cut into small pieces
2 stalks celery, finely chopped
1 cup freshly shucked corn kernels or 1 cup canned cream-style corn
1 cup light cream
2 egg yolks
Salt and pepper

Place the chicken broth, onion, potato, and celery in a 2-quart glass or ceramic casserole. Cover and cook on the highest setting for 6 minutes, until the potato and celery are very tender. Purée the soup in a blender. Add the corn.

Add ¾ cup cream and heat to simmering point for 2 minutes. Stir the remaining ¼ cup of cream with the egg yolks and add to the soup. Cook uncovered for 30 seconds. Season with salt and pepper.

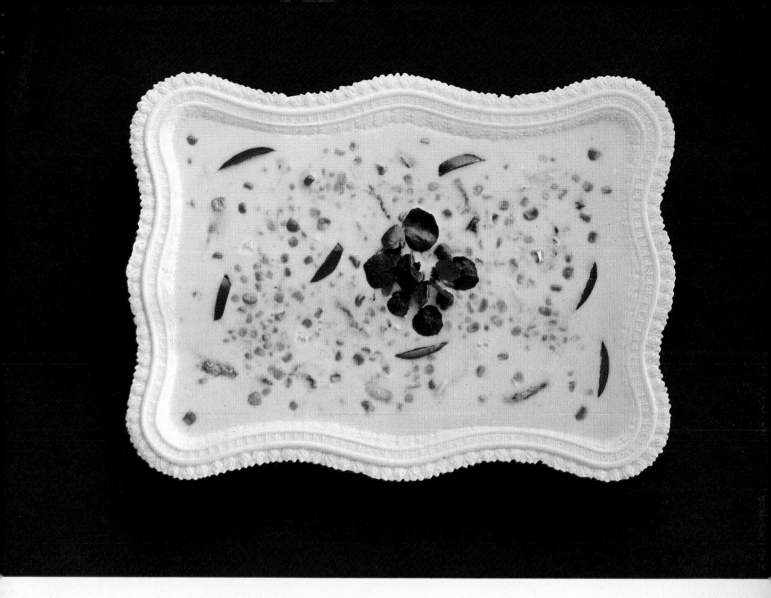

crab and corn soup

This is a soup to warm the soul of any fisherman.

Yield: 4 servings

3 tablespoons butter	**½ teaspoon salt**
⅓ cup flour	**⅛ teaspoon pepper**
2 cups milk	**¼ cup table cream**
2 cups cold water	**Slices of tomato (optional)**
1 6-ounce can crab meat	**Watercress (optional)**
12-ounce can whole-kernel corn	

Melt the butter in a 1½-quart glass or ceramic casserole for 30 seconds on the highest setting. Stir in flour with a wire whisk. While continuing to stir. Gradually stir in milk and water. Cook for 5 minutes or until thickened. During cooking stir twice with whisk to make a smooth sauce.

Drain crab and corn. Break crab meat into pieces, removing cartilage. Stir crab meat and corn into the sauce. Season with salt and pepper. Cover casserole and cook for 5 minutes on "simmer" setting. Remove from oven and stir in cream. Garnish with slices of tomato and watercress.

chicken soup

A splendid idea for lunch. All you need to go with it is a basketful of crusty rolls and some fruit for dessert.

Yield: 4 servings

1 2½-pound chicken, cut into serving pieces
4 cups water
1 onion or 2 leeks, chopped
2 carrots, diced
3 chicken bouillon cubes
1 cup fresh peas
2 tablespoons chopped parsley
Salt and pepper

Place the chicken in a 2-quart glass or ceramic casserole. Add 2 cups of water, the onion or leeks, and carrots. Cover and cook on the highest setting for 30 minutes.

Cool the chicken and discard the skin and bones. Cut the meat into small pieces and place to one side. Skim the fat from the surface of the broth in the casserole. Add the remaining 2 cups of water, the bouillon cubes, peas, and parsley. Cook for 2 minutes. Add the chicken pieces and season with salt and pepper. Continue cooking, uncovered, for 2 more minutes, until the soup is hot.

goulash soup

This soup has no added thickening, as the potato and the other ingredients give it body.

Yield: 6 servings

2 tablespoons butter
2 tablespoons oil
3 medium-size onions, sliced
1 clove garlic, finely chopped
2 teaspoons paprika
½ pound veal, ground
¼ pound pork, ground
4 cups stock (can be made with 4 bouillon cubes and 4 cups boiling water)
Salt and pepper
2 medium-size potatoes, sliced
3 small tomatoes, chopped
6 thin slices French bread

Heat butter and oil in a 3-quart glass or ceramic casserole on the highest setting for 20 seconds. Add onions and garlic and fry for 2 minutes. Add paprika and cook for 30 seconds. Stir in the ground meats, and cook for 2 minutes.
Gradually add the stock, and season to taste. Cover and cook on highest setting for 5 minutes. Add potato and tomato, and cook covered for 8 minutes longer, until the potatoes are soft. Toast bread in toaster or in a broiler until crisp and brown. Serve with the soup.

goulash soup

peanut soup

This country recipe is just as popular in the city.

Yield: 6 servings

1½-pound chicken
1 large onion, peeled and thinly sliced
1 teaspoon salt
6 whole black peppercorns
2 tablespoons unsalted butter

4 ounces salted peanuts
3 ounces dry sherry
1¼ cups milk
½ cup whipping cream

Cut the chicken into 3 or 4 pieces, removing the fat, and place in a 2½-quart glass or ceramic casserole with half the onion slices. Add salt, pepper, and 6 cups of water. Cover and cook on the highest setting for 30 minutes. Cool stock.

Heat butter in a 2-quart glass or ceramic casserole for 20 seconds. Add the remaining onions and cook for 2 minutes to soften. Rub the peanuts in a cloth to get rid of the salt. Place the peanuts, onion slices, and butter in the blender. Blend until the nuts are finely chopped. Strain the cooled stock; skim off fat. Add nuts and onions to the stock. Place in a saucepan. Cover and simmer for 15 minutes. Taste, and add more seasoning if necessary. Stir in the sherry and milk, and cook for 4 minutes.

Cover pan and refrigerate overnight. Just before serving, add the cream. Heat to simmering point but do not allow the soup to boil. Serve garnished with chopped parsley and finely chopped peanuts.

cream of broccoli soup

All cream soups are made in a similar way. Cream of asparagus soup can be made by substituting asparagus for broccoli.

Yield: 6 servings

1½ pounds broccoli
1 onion, finely chopped
1 carrot, sliced
2 stalks celery with the leaves
2 potatoes, peeled and chopped
1 teaspoon salt
3 cups chicken broth
1 cup light cream
½ cup thinly sliced boiled ham, diced
½ cup sour cream

Discard the lower third of the broccoli stems and chop the remaining part into small pieces. Place in a 2-quart glass or ceramic casserole with the onion, carrot, celery, potatoes, salt, and chicken broth. Cover and cook on the highest setting for 10 minutes, until the broccoli is tender.

Purée the soup in a blender. Add the cream and ham and heat (highest setting) for 5 minutes, until very hot. Serve with a spoonful of sour cream.

peanut soup

scottish hot pot

Yield: 6 servings

2 pounds lamb shoulder	2 carrots, diced
6 cups beef bouillon	1 turnip, diced
1 teaspoon salt	1 scallion, white and green parts, thinly sliced
½ teaspoon pepper	
2 onions, sliced	1 small cauliflower divided into florets
2 tablespoons butter	1 10-ounce package frozen peas
2 teaspoons flour	½ cup sherry
1 stalk celery, diced	2 tablespoons finely chopped parsley

In a 3-quart glass or ceramic casserole place meat, bouillon, salt, pepper, and onions. Cook on "simmer" setting for 30 minutes. Remove from oven. Cut meat into serving pieces. Heat 2 tablespoons butter in a 1-quart glass bowl at highest setting for 20 seconds. Brown meat in butter for 3 minutes and sprinkle with flour. Return meat to the stock and add celery, carrots, turnip, and scallion. Continue cooking for 15 minutes. Add cauliflower and peas to soup and cook for 8 minutes. Before serving, correct seasoning and sprinkle with parsley.

shrimp and mushroom soup

Creamy and full of textures and flavors, this soup is equally fine served hot or cold.

Yield: 6 servings

¾ pound small mushroom caps
1 small onion, finely chopped
½ small cucumber, peeled and chopped into pieces the size of the mushroom caps
1 tablespoon lemon juice
2 tablespoons white vermouth
2 tablespoons oil
1 pound small fresh shrimps with shells on
2 tablespoons butter
2 tablespoons flour
2½ cups milk
1 cup light cream
Salt and pepper

Place the mushroom caps, onion, cucumber pieces, and lemon juice in a small glass bowl. Add the white vermouth. Cover and cook on the highest setting for 2 minutes. Oil a plate. Place the shrimps on the plate. Sprinkle with oil and cook for 2 minutes (highest setting used throughout). Stir the shrimps to rearrange them after 1 minute. Peel the shrimps.

Heat the butter for 30 seconds. Stir in the flour and cook for 20 seconds. Stir in the milk and cream. Cook for 4 minutes. Stir briskly with a wire whisk. Add the mushroom mixture and the shrimps. Season with salt and pepper. Serve hot (reheat if necessary), or chill for 4 hours before serving.

scottish hot pot

eggs

Boiled Eggs

Eggs cannot be boiled in the microwave oven because the microwave energy causes a rapid expansion of gases within the confined space of the shell. At the point that the shell can no longer accommodate the increased volume, the egg "explodes" into fragments. Even if this does not happen while the egg is in the oven, it continues to cook for a moment and can break into tiny pieces afterward. This is not likely to cause any great harm either to the oven or to you, but it is somewhat startling, a waste of the egg, and a great nuisance to clean up.

Fried Eggs

The yolks of fried eggs cook more rapidly than the whites in the microwave oven. For this reason the eggs should be covered with a piece of waxed paper, and the steam that is trapped between the eggs and the paper will cause the whites to set. Though it is possible to cook several eggs at one time, it is faster to cook each one separately. In fact, if you are cooking more than 4 eggs, it is faster to use a frying pan on top of the stove. Remember that the eggs will continue to cook after they are removed from the microwave oven, so take them out while they are still slightly undercooked. The yolks of eggs that are to be fried must be pierced with a fork to prevent them from exploding through their thin covering membrane.

To fry 1 egg, heat 1 tablespoon of butter on a plate for 25 seconds. Break the egg onto the plate and cut a cross in the yolk, using the tips of the tines of a fork. Cook on "roast" setting for 1 minute. Cook 2 eggs for 2 minutes and 4 eggs for 4 minutes. Rotate the plate one-quarter of a turn after 2 minutes.

Poached Eggs

Poached eggs are very successfully cooked in the microwave oven. The yolks must be pierced before cooking to prevent them from "exploding." Heat 2 cups of water in a 4-cup glass measuring cup on the highest setting for 4 minutes. Add ¼ teaspoon salt and 1 teaspoon vinegar. Slide the egg into the water and cook on "roast" setting for 1 minute. Cook 2 eggs for 2 minutes. It is very risky to attempt to cook more than 2 eggs at a time. For some reason that I have been totally unable to fathom, the presence of a third or fourth egg sometimes causes all the eggs to leap out of the poaching water and hurl themselves against the walls of the oven. Though it does not happen every time, it happens often enough that it just seems easier to cook more than 2 eggs on top of the stove.

Scrambled Eggs

If you have no alternative method of cooking other than the microwave oven (some people use only microwave ovens in second homes), then you will have no choice but to use the microwave oven for making scrambled eggs. Prepare scrambled eggs as you normally would, with or without the addition of milk, and cook 2 scrambled eggs in a cereal bowl on "roast" setting for 2 minutes. Stir the eggs with a fork after 1 minute or the center will be undercooked. Cook 4 eggs for 5 minutes, stirring the eggs twice. As the texture of eggs scrambled in the microwave oven is undeniably changed, you may prefer to cook them in a frying pan on top of the conventional stove.

Baked Eggs

Though some claim to be able to bake eggs in the microwave oven, I have been totally unsuccessful in this area and find the whole scheme fraught with hazards that inevitably result in levitating eggs and similar phenomena. I recommend that eggs be baked in the conventional oven or that you have a roll and butter instead.

spanish eggs

This simple brunch or supper dish is a good way to use up leftovers. Chicken can be used instead of pork.

Yield: 4 servings

1 tablespoon oil
¼ small onion, finely chopped
1 clove garlic, finely chopped
½ green pepper, finely chopped
½ cup cooked pork, diced
½ cup cooked ham, diced
2 tablespoons flour

¾ cup chicken broth
½ teaspoon basil
1 tomato, peeled, seeded, and chopped
Salt and pepper
2 tablespoons butter
4 eggs

Heat the oil in an 8-inch glass pie plate. Add the onion, garlic, and green pepper and cook on the highest setting for 1 minute. Add the pork and ham. Stir in the flour and add the chicken broth and basil. Cook 3 minutes. Add the tomato and cook 1 minute. Season with salt and pepper.

Heat the butter on a plate. Break the eggs onto the plate and cut a cross in the yolks with a fork. Cook the eggs on "roast" setting for 4 minutes, until set. Slide the eggs on top of the pork mixture and decorate the edges of the plate with parsley if you wish.

deviled eggs mornay

This exciting egg dish is perfect for your microwave oven.

Yield: 4 servings

2 tablespoons butter
2 tablespoons flour
1¼ cups milk
½ teaspoon salt
¼ teaspoon pepper
1½ cups grated cheddar cheese
1 cup cooked pasta shells

6 hard-boiled eggs
1 teaspoon dry mustard
½ teaspoon curry powder
2 tablespoons butter, melted
3 or 4 green olives, sliced
3 or 4 tablespoons cream

Melt the butter in a 1-quart measuring glass for 20 seconds on the highest setting. Stir in flour with a wire whisk. Stir in milk gradually. Cook for 3 minutes or until thick. During cooking stir twice with whisk to give a smooth sauce. Season with salt and pepper. Add ½ cup of grated cheese and the cooked pasta. Place in an ovenproof dish and keep it warm in a conventional oven. Cut eggs in half lengthwise and remove yolks. Mix yolks with mustard, curry powder, melted butter, and salt and pepper to taste. Put mixture into egg-white halves. Cover with Mornay sauce. Arrange sliced olives on top of the sauce. Top with and sprinkle with remaining cheese. Cook uncovered on highest setting for 2 minutes to melt cheese. Serve immediately.

deviled eggs mornay

eggs with mustard sauce

A quick brunch to serve either alone or with crisp bacon and freshly made buttered toast.

Yield: 4 servings

6 hard-boiled eggs
2 tablespoons butter
2 tablespoons flour
1¼ cups beef or chicken broth
2 teaspoons Dijon mustard
2 tablespoons finely chopped parsley

Slice the eggs and place in a shallow buttered glass or ceramic baking dish. Heat the butter in a glass measuring cup on the highest setting. Stir in the flour. Add the broth and return to the oven for 2 minutes, until hot. Stir in the mustard and parsley.

Pour the sauce over the eggs and cook on ''roast'' setting for 2 minutes.

34

meats

Cooking Meats

As a general guide allow 6 minutes per pound for rare meats; 7 minutes per pound for medium meats, and 8 minutes per pound for well-done meats. Remember that all foods continue to cook after they are removed from the oven. Check the temperature of a roast after it is removed from the oven. The temperature will continue to rise 10 to 20 degrees, depending on the density of the meat. Rest small roasts 10 minutes before carving; rest larger roasts, more than 3 pounds in weight, for 15 minutes.

Do not salt the surface of meat before cooking, as salt distorts the pattern of the microwaves, slowing down the cooking and toughening the surface. Arrange foods in a circle or, as in the case of frankfurters, with a 1-inch space between each frankfurter, as microwaves are attracted to the edges of the food. Cook chicken breasts in the center of a baking dish and arrange the legs around the sides of the dish.

35

Roasting

No book can hope to cover every variable, so please use your own judgment in cooking with the microwave oven. Check the internal temperature of cooked meats with a meat thermometer, and taste vegetables to be sure they are tender before serving. Bear in mind that prime meat will be more tender and cook more rapidly than a piece of choice meat. The fat in well-marbled meat melts during the cooking, keeping the meat bathed in moisture. The moisture in turn attracts the microwaves, causing it to cook quickly.

Tough meat that consists of fibrous tissue should be braised, pot-roasted, or stewed, because even the microwave oven cannot turn a chuck steak into a succulent roast beef.

Meats without bones cook more rapidly in the microwave oven than do meats containing bone.

Meats at room temperature will cook more rapidly than those at refrigeration temperature. All the recipes in this book assume that the food is at refrigeration temperature.

Frozen Meat

If the meat is frozen, defrost it. Do not try to cook it in its frozen state, because the outside will become overcooked while the center may remain solidly frozen. As in all cooking in the microwave oven, the heat must penetrate the food layer by layer.

Seasoning the Meat

Roast meats cannot be salted while they are cooking, because salt deflects the microwaves, slowing down the cooking process and toughening the surface layer. However, you can salt the roast immediately after it is taken from the oven and left to rest. Meat can be seasoned with pepper, herbs, and spices before cooking. (Do not use blended herbs such as garlic salt.) Roast meats also may be brushed with soy sauce while they are cooking. Soy sauce gives a salty taste and darkens the color of the roast, giving it an appetizing appearance.

Placing the Roast in the Oven

A special roasting rack can be purchased for use in the microwave oven. If you do not have one, place the roast on an inverted saucer set in a large glass or ceramic baking dish. Do not place the roast directly in the baking dish or the underside will fry in its own fat.

Protecting the Roast

Unevenly shaped roasts will cook unevenly, just as they do in the conventional oven. To prevent thinner parts of the roast from becoming overcooked, wrap them loosely with lightweight aluminum foil halfway through the cooking process. Be sure the foil does not touch the sides of the oven, or it will cause arcing effects and can damage the oven mechanism.

Rotating the Roast

All food cooks more evenly in the microwave oven when it is rotated. Estimate the total cooking time of the roast and cook it for half the time with the fat side down (or breast side down if you are cooking poultry) and for the remaining time on the reverse side. Also, rotate the dish one-quarter of a turn as each quarter of the cooking time elapses.

Checking the Doneness of the Roast

A special thermometer is available for use in the microwave oven, but, if you do not have one, check the temperature of the roast with a metal thermometer after the meat is taken from the oven. The temperature will rise as much as 20 degrees during the resting time.

Resting the Roast

It is very important to allow the meat to rest for 10 to 15 minutes after it is removed from the oven. The cooking process is completed during this time, and the juices become evenly distributed, making the meat moist and flavorful. If this resting time is eliminated, the juices will pour from the meat, leaving it with a poor taste and texture. Wrap the roast in aluminum foil during the resting period so it will not become cold.

cooking meats

Food	Quantity	Directions	Time
Bacon	3 slices	Paper plate lined with folded paper towels.	3 min
	6 slices	Same as above. If cooking more than 6 slices, quicker in frying pan.	6 min
Beef stew	2½ lb	Cover and rotate casserole 4 times.	Cook on "roast" 50 min
		Reheat.	"High" 10 min
Chicken parts	1 serving	Place on ceramic plate with meaty part to side of plate. Turn and rotate halfway through cooking time.	5 min
Fish	1 serving	Place on ceramic plate. Cover with waxed paper. Rotate halfway through cooking time.	4 min
Frankfurter	1	Cook on preheated browning plate.	25 sec
Frankfurters	4	As above. Turn after 20 sec.	1 min 25 sec
Hamburger	1 (4 oz)	Cook on preheated browning plate. Make a depression in the center, or edges cook too rapidly.	4 min
Hamburgers	4 (1 lb)	As above. Turn after 2 min.	5 min
Meat loaf	1 lb	Cook in ring mold or place custard cup in center of baking dish. Rotate halfway through cooking time.	Cook 5 min Rest 5 min Cook 2 min
Sausage links and patties	1 lb	Arrange on ceramic plate. Turn and rotate halfway through cooking time.	4 min

rib roast

rolled rib roast

Large tender cuts of beef become moist and succulent when they are cooked for part of the time on the "roast" setting of the microwave oven. The texture then remains firm, and the beef is well-browned. Do not salt the beef before cooking or the surface layer will be toughened.

Yield: 8 servings

1 4-pound boneless rolled rib roast
Salt and pepper

Place the roast, fat side down, on a microwave oven roasting rack or on an inverted saucer in a glass or ceramic baking dish, to permit the fat to drain. If the roast rests directly on the baking dish, the under part will fry and then stew in its own juices.

Cook on the highest setting for 12 minutes. Turn the beef over and rotate the dish one-quarter of a turn and cook for another 12 minutes on "roast" setting. The internal temperature will read 118 to 120°F but will increase as much as 20 degrees as it stands. Season the beef with salt and pepper and cover with aluminum foil. Let the beef rest for 15 minutes before carving. This resting period is important, because if the beef is carved too quickly, it will be insufficiently cooked and the juices will pour out, leaving the meat dry and tasteless.

ground beef and noodles

It is very easy to inadvertently overcook ground beef dishes in the microwave oven because they cook very quickly. Taste the beef after 5 minutes and let it rest for 5 minutes. Taste it again and return it to the oven for another minute only if you are really sure it needs additional time.

Yield: 4 servings

1 pound ground chuck steak
1 tablespoon oil
1 onion, finely chopped
1 clove garlic, finely chopped
1 green pepper, finely chopped
½ teaspoon oregano
¼ cup beef broth

¾ cup sour cream
1 tablespoon tomato paste
2 tomatoes peeled, seeded, and chopped
1½ cups cooked noodles or macaroni
½ teaspoon salt
Freshly ground black pepper

Preheat a ceramic browning plate on the highest setting for 4 minutes. Add the beef and oil and cook for 2 minutes. Drain off any accumulated fat and transfer to a 2-quart glass or ceramic casserole. Add the onion, garlic, and green pepper to the casserole and cook for 2 minutes. Add all the remaining ingredients. Cover and cook for 5 minutes. Stir the mixture once and rotate the dish one-quarter of a turn after 3 minutes. Taste the beef and season with salt and pepper.

pot roast

A 3-pound piece of beef is pot-roasted in 2½ hours the conventional way. With a microwave oven it takes 1½ hours.

Yield: 6 servings

1 3-pound boneless chuck steak, in one piece, or cross-cut shoulder of beef

marinade

1½ cups young red wine such as Beaujolais or California Mountain red wine
2 tablespoons oil
1 onion, chopped
1 clove garlic, chopped

1 stalk celery, chopped
1 teaspoon salt
1 bay leaf
1 teaspoon thyme
3 sprigs parsley
10 peppercorns

Tie the beef at ½-inch intervals so it will keep its shape. Combine the marinade ingredients in a 2½-quart glass casserole. Place the beef in the marinade. There should be enough liquid to cover the beef. If not, it will be necessary to turn the beef from time to time. Cover and refrigerate the beef for 12 hours or up to 3 days.

Place the beef, immersed in the marinade and covered, in the microwave oven. Cook on "simmer" setting for 45 minutes. Turn the beef over. Rotate the dish one-quarter of a turn after each 20 minutes. Allow to stand for 20 minutes before slicing.

sauce for pot roast

Yield: 2 cups

2 tablespoons butter
2 tablespoons flour
1¼ cups cooking liquid from the casserole

½ cup tomato sauce
¼ cup mayonnaise
¼ teaspoon thyme

Heat the butter in a 4-cup glass measuring cup for 30 seconds on the highest setting. Stir in the flour and cook for 20 seconds. Stir in all the remaining ingredients with a wire whisk. Heat on "simmer" setting for 5 minutes.

corned beef hash

Corned beef hash made from leftover corned beef is ready to eat very quickly when it is made in the microwave oven. Cook the fried eggs separately and place on top of the hot hash.

Yield: 4 servings

1 pound ground or finely chopped corned beef
2 cups finely chopped cabbage (use a meat grinder or food processor if you have one), parboiled for 6 minutes
1 onion, finely chopped

2 boiled potatoes, diced
¼ cup tomato purée
½ teaspoon salt
Freshly ground black pepper
2 tablespoons oil
2 eggs, fried (optional)

Combine all ingredients except the oil. Pour the oil into a shallow 9-inch glass baking dish and heat for 30 seconds on the highest setting. Add the hash ingredients and cook 2 minutes. Stir the hash and cook 3 minutes. Top with fried eggs if you wish.

beef stew

Stewing beef cooks too rapidly on the highest setting of the microwave oven; all stews are much more successfully prepared at the "simmer" speed. The beef can be browned first either in a frying pan on top of the stove or on the browning plate that is supplied with the newer ovens.

Yield: 6 servings

2½ pounds boneless chuck steak
3 tablespoons oil
1 onion, finely chopped
1 clove garlic, finely chopped
2 carrots, diced
2 stalks celery, sliced

2 tablespoons flour
1½ cups beef broth
2 teaspoons tomato paste
½ teaspoon thyme
1 bay leaf

Trim the beef and cut into 1-inch cubes. Brown the cubes in hot oil and transfer to a 2-quart glass or ceramic casserole. Cook the onion, garlic, carrots, and celery in the same oil for 2 minutes. Stir in the flour and ½ cup of the beef broth. Transfer to the casserole with the beef and add the remaining broth and seasonings. Cover and cook at "simmer" setting for 50 minutes.

Cool and chill overnight; then reheat on "reheat" speed for 10 minutes. Rotate the dish and stir the stew once after 5 minutes. Discard the bay leaf before serving.

beef stewed in red wine

This is a delicious casserole meal.

Yield: 6 servings

1½ pounds boneless chuck steak, cut into 1½-inch cubes
2 tablespoons butter
1 tablespoon oil
1 large turnip, cut into 1-inch pieces
1 rutabaga, cut into 1-inch pieces
1 pound small white onions, peeled
1 pound carrots, cut into 1-inch pieces
3 tablespoons flour
1 cup beef bouillon
1 cup red wine
Dash of Worcestershire sauce
½ teaspoon peppercorns
3 bay leaves

Heat butter and oil in a 3-quart glass or ceramic casserole for 20 seconds. Brown beef, turnip, rutabaga, onions, and carrots for 4 minutes. Add flour, stir, and cook for another 2 minutes. Add bouillon, wine, Worcestershire sauce, peppercorns, and bay leaves. Cover and cook at "simmer" setting for 50 minutes. Leave overnight and reheat next day.

beef stewed in red wine

english layered-beef pudding
Yield: 6 servings

1 pound basic bread dough (may be purchased in frozen form)
1 pound ground beef
4 strips bacon, cut into small pieces
2 small onions, chopped
1 clove garlic, finely chopped
1 teaspoon salt
½ teaspoon pepper
2 tomatoes
½ cup grated cheddar cheese
2 tablespoons whipping cream

Divide dough into 6 parts and roll out each section to fit size of casserole. Combine ground beef, onion, garlic, and seasonings, and arrange between layers of dough in an oiled 2-quart glass or ceramic casserole. Top with sliced tomato, grated cheese, and cream. Cover and bake for 8 minutes on the highest setting. Turn dish one-quarter of a turn every 2 minutes. Leave pudding in the pan for 5 minutes.

chili

If you are a chili addict, you can indulge yourself in a steaming, spicy bowl of beef and beans in 10 minutes. Serve the chili on a bed of rice or in taco shells. Pour a glass of beer and have some chopped raw onions, shredded iceberg lettuce, and grated sharp cheddar cheese as a garnish if you wish.

Yield: 2 servings

½ pound ground beef
1 tablespoon oil
½ small onion, finely chopped
1 clove garlic, finely chopped
2 teaspoons chili powder
¼ teaspoon ground cumin
Dash cayenne pepper

Dash Tabasco sauce
½ cup tomato sauce
2 canned tomatoes
½ teaspoon salt
8-ounce can red kidney beans, drained

Place the ground beef in a 1-quart glass bowl. Cook for 2 minutes on the highest setting and drain any accumulated fat. Fluff the beef with a fork and put to one side. Heat the oil in a custard cup for 20 seconds on the same setting. Add the onion and garlic and cook for 1 minute. Add the chili and cumin and cook for 50 seconds. Stir these and all the remaining ingredients except the beans into the bowl with the ground beef. Cover and cook for 4 minutes. Stir in the kidney beans and cook another 2 minutes.

english layered beef pudding

skillet supper

Yield: 6 servings

½ pound ground beef
3 tablespoons oil
2 onions, sliced
1 clove garlic, minced
1 small eggplant,
   cut into ½-inch cubes
1 8-ounce can tomato sauce

1 small green pepper, chopped
½ teaspoon salt
¼ teaspoon pepper
4 ounces egg noodles,
   cooked, drained
6 eggs
¼ teaspoon cayenne pepper

Place the ground beef in a 1-quart glass bowl. Cook for 2 minutes on the highest setting and drain the accumulated fat. Stir the beef with a fork and put to one side. Heat the oil in a 12-inch glass bowl for 20 seconds on the same setting. Add the onions and garlic and cook for 1 minute. Add ground beef, eggplant, tomatoes, green pepper, salt, and pepper. Cover and cook for 4 minutes. Add cooked noodles and mix thoroughly. With back of spoon make 6 hollows in meat mixture. Break an egg into each hollow. Cover tightly with a lid or plastic wrap. Cook eggs on "roast" setting for about 8 minutes or until eggs are cooked to desired doneness. Let stand, covered, for 2 minutes before serving.

macaroni cauliflower casserole

macaroni-cauliflower casserole

This is cauliflower cheese with a difference for an economical and filling meal.

Yield: 4 servings

2 tablespoons butter
1 small onion, finely chopped
½ pound ground beef
3 tablespoons catsup
¼ cup water
½ teaspoon salt
⅛ teaspoon pepper
1 small cauliflower,
   broken into florets

4 ounces elbow macaroni
   (about 1 cup)
2 tablespoons butter
2 tablespoons flour
1¼ cups milk
1 egg, lightly beaten
1 cup cheddar cheese, grated
To garnish: parsley sprigs

Heat 2 tablespoons butter in a 1-quart glass casserole on the highest setting for 20 seconds. Add onion and ground beef and fry for 2 minutes. Drain fat and add catsup, water, salt, and pepper; cook on "reheat" setting for 5 minutes.

In a separate covered glass casserole cook cauliflower in ½ cup water for 8 minutes. Rotate dish one-quarter of a turn halfway through the cooking period. Remove cauliflower with a slotted spoon.

The eggs can be cooked in the microwave oven. (See note on preparing fried eggs.)

Bring 2 cups of water, 1 tablespoon cooking oil, and 1 teaspoon salt to a full boil in a 2-quart glass casserole on highest setting. Stir in macaroni. Recover, and cook on "defrost" setting for 10 to 12 minutes. Drain well.

Melt the remaining 2 tablespoons of butter in a glass dish on the highest setting for 20 seconds. Stir in flour with a wire whisk. Gradually stir in the milk. Cook for 3 minutes or until thick. Stir twice during cooking to give a smooth sauce. Season to taste. Remove from heat and stir in beaten egg and ½ cup of cheese.

Mix macaroni and cauliflower with the prepared sauce. Oil a 3-quart glass casserole and add ground beef mixture. Top with macaroni and cauliflower in cheese sauce. Sprinkle with remaining grated cheese. Cook on "reheat" setting for 5 minutes or until hot. Place in a preheated conventional oven at 400° F for the last 10 minutes to brown the topping. Garnish with parsley.

tagliatelle bolognese

This Italian dish is delicious from your microwave oven.

Yield: 4 to 6 servings

meat sauce

2 tablespoons butter	1 bay leaf
1 onion, finely chopped	½ cup cup beef bouillon
1 carrot, diced	½ teaspoon salt
1 stalk celery, diced	⅛ teaspoon pepper
1 clove garlic (optional), finely chopped	1 teaspoon sugar
2 strips bacon, diced	¾ pound Tagliatelle or other pasta
½ pound ground beef	⅓ cup grated Parmesan cheese
1 8-ounce can tomato sauce	

Heat butter in a 3-quart glass casserole on the highest setting for 20 seconds. Add vegetables and diced bacon. Cook for 2 minutes. Add ground beef and cook on highest setting for 7 minutes; drain. Stir in tomato sauce, bay leaf, bouillon, salt, pepper, and sugar. Cover with a glass lid and cook on "reheat" setting for 7 minutes. Taste and add more seasoning if necessary. Remove the bay leaf.

In a 3-quart covered glass casserole, bring 6 cups of water, 1 tablespoon cooking oil, and 1 teaspoon salt to a full boil on highest setting. Stir in pasta and re-cover. Cook on "defrost" setting for 14 minutes or until tender. Drain and rinse thoroughly. Turn into a hot serving dish, pour cooked meat sauce into the center, and sprinkle with Parmesan cheese.

Picture on next page: tagliatelle bolognese

lamb chops braised in red wine

The presentation of all foods is of great importance. Even chops can look sensational when served on an attractive platter, garnished with crisp watercress and the contrasting colors of boiled parslied potatoes and tomato halves.

Yield: 6 servings

6 thick loin lamb chops
2 tablespoons oil
1 onion, finely chopped
1 clove garlic, finely chopped
2 tomatoes, chopped
½ cup tomato purée
1 cup red wine

½ cup beef broth
1 teaspoon basil
1 bay leaf
Salt and pepper
1 tablespoon butter
2 tablespoons flour

Trim the lamb chops. Heat the microwave browning plate for 4 minutes on the highest setting. Add the oil and cook the chops, one at a time, for 1 minute on each side. Transfer the chops to a 2-quart glass or ceramic casserole and add all the remaining ingredients except the butter and flour. Cover and cook on "roast" setting for 30 minutes. Remove the chops. Arrange them on a hot serving plate and keep them warm while preparing the sauce.

Strain the liquid from the casserole. Heat the butter on the highest setting for 30 seconds. Stir in the flour and cook for 30 seconds. Stir in the strained cooking liquid with a wire whisk. Taste, add salt and pepper, and reheat if necessary. Serve the sauce over the lamb chops or separately.

lamb pilaf

Here's an interesting way of preparing leftover lamb. There is merely a hint of the spices but there are many textures and tastes to think about as the food is eaten.

Yield: 6 servings

2 tablespoons oil
1 onion, finely chopped
¼ teaspoon allspice
¼ teaspoon cinnamon
¼ teaspoon thyme
2 cups cooked lamb, cut into bite-size pieces
3 cups cooked rice
1 tomato, peeled, seeded, and chopped
1 cup cooked sliced zucchini or other green vegetable
⅓ cup slivered almonds
⅓ cup raisins, soaked in hot water for 5 minutes and drained
½ cup beef broth

Heat the oil in a 1½-quart glass or ceramic casserole on the highest setting. Fry the onion in the oil for 1 minute. Stir in the spices and cook for 30 seconds. Stir in all the remaining ingredients and cook for 8 minutes. Rotate the dish one-quarter of a turn every 2 minutes.

butterfly leg of lamb

Ask the butcher to remove the bone from the lamb and "butterfly" it. You will then have a flattish piece of meat to serve 6 people. The meat will be cooked in less than 20 minutes.

Yield: 6 servings

1 3-pound leg of lamb, weighed after the bone is removed
1 slice bread, broken into 6 pieces
½ cup parsley
1 teaspoon rosemary
3 tablespoons butter
2 cloves garlic, finely chopped
Salt and pepper

Place the lamb, fat side down, on a microwave oven roasting rack or on top of an inverted saucer set in a glass baking dish.

Place the bread, parsley, and rosemary in a blender and blend until finely chopped. Spread the mixture on the surface of the lamb.

Heat the butter and garlic in a custard cup on the highest setting for 40 seconds. Drizzle the garlic butter over the lamb.

Cook the lamb on the highest setting for 10 minutes. Rotate the dish one-quarter of a turn and cook on "roast" setting for 8 minutes. Season with salt and pepper and leave to rest for 10 minutes before slicing.

roast lamb

For rare lamb cook for 8 minutes per pound. For medium lamb cook for 9 minutes per pound. For well-done lamb cook for 10 minutes per pound.

To acheive moist lamb with excellent taste, texture, and color, the roast should be cooked for the second half of the estimated time at a slower speed. If your oven does not have a "roast" setting, place a glass of hot water in the oven during the second half of the cooking time. The water will deflect some of the microwave energy and slow the cooking process.

Yield: 6 servings

1 5-pound leg of lamb with the bone	**1 teaspoon rosemary**
3 cloves garlic	**Freshly ground pepper**
3 tablespoons butter, melted	**Salt**

Trim the excess fat from the lamb. Make a series of slits in the surface of the lamb with the point of a sharp knife. Cut the garlic into slivers and insert tiny pieces of garlic into the slits. Brush the lamb with melted butter. Press the rosemary onto the surface of the lamb and season with pepper.

Place the lamb fat side down on a rack or on an inverted saucer set in a glass or ceramic baking dish. Cook on the highest setting for 20 minutes. Turn the lamb on its other side and brush with butter. Cook on "roast" setting or place a glass of hot water in the oven for 20 minutes longer (150°F) for rare lamb; 25 more minutes (160°F) for medium lamb, and 30 more minutes (170°F) for well-done lamb. Season with salt and cover with aluminum foil. Allow to stand for 15 minutes before carving. The temperature will continue to rise during this resting time.

lamb stew

To speed preparation and help blend flavors, cover stews.

Yield: 4 servings

1 pound boneless lamb,
    cut into 6 pieces
1 tablespoon flour
2 teaspoons salt
¼ teaspoon pepper
3 tablespoons oil

1 cup white wine
1 tablespoon tomato paste
2 cups water
1 clove garlic, minced
½ pound carrots, cubed
2 turnips, cubed

¼ pound fresh
    green beans
¼ pound fresh
    green peas
6 small potatoes
1 onion, diced

Combine flour, salt, and pepper. Coat lamb in seasoned flour. Place oil in a 2-quart glass casserole with meat. Cover and cook on "roast" setting for 10 minutes. Add wine, tomato paste, water, and garlic and bring to boil on highest setting. Add all vegetables except peas and cook covered on "simmer" setting for 35 minutes. Add peas and cook 4 minutes longer.

lamb stew

lamb chop stew

lamb-chop stew

Your microwave oven allows preparation of this dish in just a fraction of the ordinary time.

Yield: 6 servings

2 cups chicken broth	**6 lamb chops**
1 bay leaf	**2 tablespoons oil**
2 whole cloves	**2 stalks celery, sliced**
¼ teaspoon peppercorns	**2 large onions, sliced**
¼ pound pearl barley	**1 pound carrots, sliced**
Bouquet garni (1 bay leaf and 3 sprigs	**2 leeks or 1 additional onion, sliced**
of parsley tied with string or thread)	**3 tablespoons flour**

Heat oil in microwave browning plate for 4 minutes on highest setting. Cook the chops, one at a time, for 1 minute on each side. Transfer the chops to a 2½-quart glass or ceramic casserole and add all the sliced vegetables. Cook combination for 2 minutes. Stir flour and bouillon. Gradually add flour and bouillon, bay leaf, cloves, peppercorns, pearl barley, and bouquet garni. Cover and cook on "simmer" setting for 50 minutes. Remove bouquet garni and serve.

lamb shanks

All stewed meats are spectacularly successful when they are cooked in the microwave oven, and the preparation time for this particular dish is reduced by one-third.

Yield: 4 servings
>**3 tablespoons oil**
>**4 lamb shanks, weighing approximately 12 ounces each**
>**3 tablespoons flour**
>**1½ cups beef broth**
>**1 teaspoon rosemary**
>**1 onion, finely chopped**
>**2 cloves garlic, finely chopped**
>**4 carrots, chopped into 1-inch pieces**
>**1 8½-ounce package frozen peas**

Heat the oil in a skillet and brown the lamb shanks on all sides. Transfer to a 2½-quart glass or ceramic casserole. Stir the flour into the oil. Add the beef broth gradually, stirring to form a smooth sauce. Add all the remaining ingredients except the peas, and pour over the lamb. Cover and cook on "roast" setting for 50 minutes. Add the peas and continue cooking for 10 minutes at the same setting.

lamb chops with gooseberry-mint sauce

This is a quick meal with a sauce to lift it out of the ordinary.

Yield: 2 servings
>**2 tablespoons oil**
>**4 small lamb chops**
>**½ teaspoon salt**
>**⅛ teaspoon pepper**
>**Watercress for garnish**

sauce

>**6 to 8 ounces fresh gooseberries or 1 pound canned gooseberries, drained**
>**2 tablespoons water**
>**1 tablespoon butter**
>**3 tablespoons sugar**
>**1 tablespoon chopped fresh mint**

Heat oil in microwave browning plate for 4 minutes on highest setting. Cook the chops, one at a time, for 1 minute on each side. Place chops in a 2-quart glass baking dish. Cover and cook on "roast" setting for 4 minutes. Season with salt and pepper. Arrange on a serving dish; garnish with trimmed watercress. Serve sauce separately.

To prepare sauce: Wash gooseberries and place in a glass bowl with water, butter, and sugar. Cover and cook on highest setting for 2 minutes or until the fruit is tender. Put in a blender and purée until smooth. Before serving heat the purée on "simmer" setting for 1 minute. Stir in the finely chopped mint.

Picture on next page: lamb chops with gooseberry mint sauce

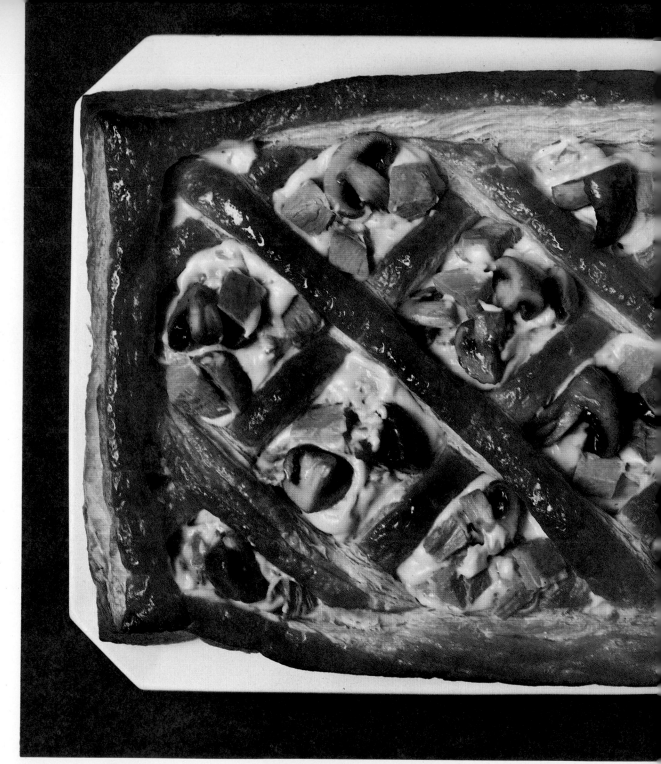

ham and mushroom pastry slice

Here is a new combination of familiar ingredients.

Yield: 4 servings

1 recipe double pie crust	¼ pound mushrooms, chopped
2 tablespoons butter	1½ cups cooked ham, diced
¼ cup flour	¼ teaspoon pepper
¾ cup milk	1 small egg, beaten

Prepare pastry. Melt butter in 2-quart glass or ceramic casserole for 20 seconds. Stir in flour with a wire whisk. Add milk gradually while continuing to stir. Cook for 3 minutes or until thickened to a sauce. During cooking, stir twice with whisk to ensure a smooth sauce. Stir mushrooms, ham, and pepper into the sauce.

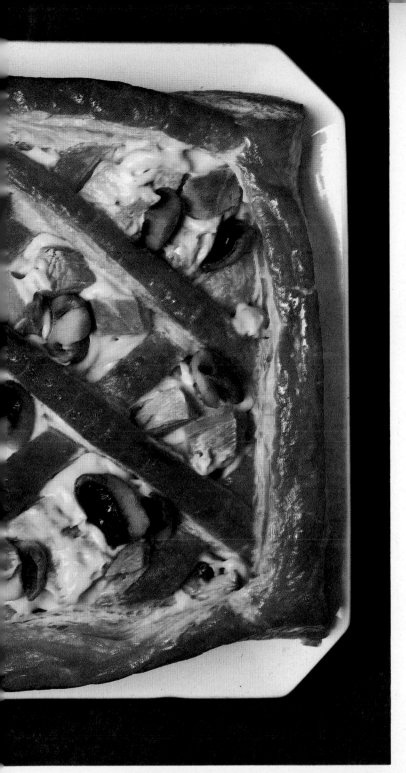

ham and mushroom pastry slice

Roll pastry into an oblong shape, 24 x 8 inches. Cut in half widthwise. Trim edges. Place one piece of pastry on a shallow rectangular glass casserole. Fold the other piece in half; cut out the center to leave a 1-inch border. Cut the center piece into strips.

Spoon sauce onto pastry base, spreading carefully to within 1 inch of the edges. Moisten edge of pastry and lay strips across the sauce. Place pastry border around the edge. Press to seal. Brush pastry with beaten egg. Cook in oven on highest setting for 8 minutes. Rotate casserole one-quarter of a turn after 4 minutes. Pie crust will not brown unless oven has a special unit. Place casserole in a conventional oven, preheated to 375°F for 10 to 15 minutes to brown crust.

baking ham

For ham weighing 3 pounds or less allow 10 minutes per pound. For ham weighing 3 to 10 pounds allow 9 minutes per pound. Check the internal temperature of the ham with an oven thermometer 10 minutes after it has been taken from the microwave oven.

baked ham with cumberland sauce

A ham, presented with a fruity Cumberland sauce, makes a popular dinner for family or friends. The sauce can be served with the ham or passed separately, and the ham itself may be served hot or cold. Allow 10 minutes cooking time to the pound.

Yield: 6 servings

1 3-pound fully cooked ham

glaze

1 jar (8 ounces) apricot preserves

Remove the rind from the ham and score the fat with a sharp wet knife to form a diamond pattern. Place the ham in the oven on a roasting rack or on an inverted saucer set in a glass baking dish. Place the ham fat side down. Cook on "roast" setting for 15 minutes. Turn the ham over and remove from the oven.

Remove the lid from the apricot preserves and heat in the jar on the highest setting for 5 minutes. Force the hot preserves through a strainer and brush the clear liquid over the ham. Rotate the dish one-quarter of a turn and continue cooking on "roast" setting for another 15 minutes. Allow the ham to stand for 15 minutes before slicing.

cumberland sauce for ham

Yield: 1¼ cups
Rind and juice of 1 orange
1 tablespoon lemon juice
3 scallions, finely chopped
½ cup port wine
½ cup red currant jelly
½ teaspoon powdered ginger
1 teaspoon dry mustard powder, dissolved in
1 tablespoon cold water

Peel the thin, colored part of the orange and cut into tiny julienne strips the length of a matchstick and half of the width. Squeeze the orange into a 4-cup glass measuring cup and add the orange rind to the orange juice. Add the lemon juice and scallions. Cook in the microwave oven on the highest setting for 3 minutes. Stir in the remaining ingredients. Cook uncovered in the microwave oven for 3 minutes, until the red currant jelly has dissolved.

Serve the sauce cold. It is traditionally a rather thin sauce.

baked ham with mustard crust

This beautiful-looking ham is very easy to prepare and is a good choice for a large buffet party. Allow 9 minutes to the pound for a ham weighing 5 to 10 pounds.

Yield: 10 servings

1 5-pound fully cooked ham	1½ cups freshly made
1 jar (8 ounces) apricot preserves	bread crumbs
2 teaspoons dry English mustard powder	¼ cup parsley
2 teaspoons Dijon mustard	¼ cup chopped chives
1 tablespoon cornstarch	1 teaspoon marjoram
2 egg yolks	3 tablespoons butter, melted

Score the ham fat in a diamond pattern after removing the rind. Place the ham, fat side down, in a microwave oven roasting rack or set on 2 saucers inverted in a glass baking dish. Cook on "roast" setting for 25 minutes. Remove the ham from the oven.

Remove the lid from the apricot preserves and heat in the jar on the highest setting for 5 minutes. Force the hot preserves through a strainer and brush the clear liquid over the ham. Rotate the dish one-quarter of a turn and continue cooking on "roast" setting for 20 minutes. Remove from the oven and check the temperature with a meat thermometer. The reading should be 150°F. The temperature will rise 10 degrees as it stands. Leave the ham to rest for 15 minutes.

Preheat the conventional oven to 375°F. Combine the mustard powder, mustard, and cornstarch. Stir in the egg yolks. Spread the mixture over the surface of the ham.

Place the bread crumbs, parsley, chives, and marjoram in a blender and blend until the herbs are finely chopped. Press the bread crumbs lightly over the mustard covering. Place the ham on a roasting rack. Drizzle with melted butter. Cook in the preheated oven for 20 minutes until the crumbs are lightly browned.

sugar-baked ham

A covered dish is not required during the roasting of this ham, but, during the standing period, a cover is necessary to assure even heating and cooking.

Yield: 6 servings

3-pound boneless ready-to-eat ham	1 tablespoon corn oil
2 bay leaves	⅓ cup brown sugar
6 peppercorns	Watercress for garnish
3 cups water	

Place ham in a large glass casserole. Add bay leaves and peppercorns. On highest setting, bring to a boil. Reduce heat to "simmer" setting and cook for 20 minutes. Remove from liquid and remove rind from ham. Brush ham with oil and sprinkle the surface of the ham with sugar. Cook on "roast" setting for 15 minutes. Cover and let stand for another 15 minutes before slicing. Garnish with watercress.

Picture on next page: (clockwise from top left) *chicken pie*
sugar-baked ham
liver pâté

sausage and egg roll

To keep sausage moist, cook in covered glass dish. Excess grease can be drained easily. Place smaller amounts on paper towels or napkins to absorb grease.

Yield: 4 servings

		1 pound pork sausage meat
2 cups flour	¼ cup shortening	4 large eggs, hard-boiled
Pinch of salt	¼ cup butter	Milk, to brush

Sift flour and salt into a mixing bowl. Cut in shortening and butter, using a pastry blender or two knives. Stir in just enough water to give a firm dough. Roll out to a rectangle and trim to about 9 x 11 inches. Place in an ungreased glass baking dish.

Cook sausage meat in a covered glass dish on highest setting for 6 minutes. Pour off grease. Spread sausage meat in a rectangle 11 x 4 inches on center of pastry. Remove shell from eggs, slice, and place in a line down the center of sausage meat. Brush one long edge of pastry with water and fold over so edges meet. Seal and flute edges. Make a diagonal cut in the top pastry. Brush pastry top with milk. Cook on "roast" setting for 9 minutes. Cool.

stuffed sausages

These may be prepared the day before.

Yield: 12 to 16 sausages

1 pound fresh sausage links	¼ cup butter
4 tablespoons chutney	⅓ cup almonds, chopped

Preheat browning grill in oven on highest setting. Place sausages on grill and cook on highest setting for 8 minutes. Turn sausage over halfway through cooking. Drain off fat and cool. Chop any large pieces of chutney. Work chutney into butter. Cut a slit down the side of the sausage from end to end and open like a book. Spoon in a little chutney stuffing, partly close sausage, and dip the stuffed side into a saucer of almonds. Arrange on a dish and serve cold.

pork with rice and oranges

This is an interesting way to serve leftover roast pork.

Yield: 4 servings

2 cups diced roast pork	¼ cup raisins soaked for 5 minutes
2 tablespoons oil	in hot water and drained
1 small onion, finely chopped	2 cups chicken broth
1 cup long-grain rice	½ cup orange juice
1 teaspoon paprika	1 tablespoon butter
1 teaspoon cinnamon	Salt and pepper
1 teaspoon cumin	Grated rind of 2 oranges
½ cup pine nuts or slivered almonds	2 oranges, sliced

Trim the pork of all fat. Heat the oil in a 2-quart glass or ceramic casserole on the highest setting for 20 seconds. Add the onion and cook for 1 minute. Add the rice and cook for 1 minute. Stir once. Rotate the dish one-quarter of a turn and cook 1 more minute. Add all remaining ingredients except the sliced oranges. Add the pork. Cover and cook for 10 minutes. Let stand 10 minutes. Garnish with sliced oranges heated in the microwave oven for 1 minute.

casserole of pork and apples

Pork is at its best when it is cooked slowly, so prepare this casserole on the "roast" setting. It will be ready to eat in half the conventional cooking time. Cumin gives the pork an unusually good flavor. Serve with cauliflower and crusty bread.

Yield: 6 servings

3 pounds boneless pork loin cut into 1½-inch cubes
2 tablespoons oil
4 leeks, washed and sliced, or 2 onions, sliced
2 green cooking apples, peeled, cored, and sliced
1 teaspoon cumin powder or curry powder
2 tablespoons flour
1¼ cups apple cider
¼ cup apple brandy or white vermouth
1 teaspoon salt
Freshly ground black pepper

Brown the pork in hot oil in a skillet and transfer the cubes to a casserole. Cook the leeks or onions and apples in the same oil for 3 minutes until softened. Stir in the cumin or curry powder and cook 1 minute. Stir in the flour and all the remaining ingredients. Transfer to a 2-quart glass or ceramic casserole. Cover and cook in the microwave oven for 1 hour on "roast" setting. Rotate the dish one-quarter of a turn after 30 minutes. Allow to rest 10 minutes before serving.

pork roast with prunes

Yield: 4 servings

12 large dried prunes	**1½ teaspoon salt**
1 cup beef bouillon	**2 large red apples**
4 pounds boneless pork roast,	**¾ cup water**
cut into 1-inch slices	**1 tablespoon sugar**
½ teaspoon pepper	**½ teaspoon lemon juice**
¼ teaspoon ground ginger	**Parsley, for garnish**

Soak prunes in bouillon overnight. Remove and pit. Reserve bouillon and 4 prunes. Mix remaining prunes with pepper and ginger. Push them in between the slices of the roast. Place pork on a microwave oven roasting rack or on an inverted saucer in a glass baking dish to permit the fat to drain. Cook on the highest setting for 24 minutes. Turn roast over and rotate the dish one-quarter of a turn and cook for another 20 to 24 minutes on "roast" setting. Remove from oven and transfer roast to serving platter. Sprinkle with salt and cover with aluminum foil. Let the roast rest for 15 minutes before serving. The pork will continue cooking.

Pour off fat from roasting pan. Add reserved bouillon. Bring to boil on highest setting for 2 minutes. Stir and continue cooking to reduce juices.

Core apples. Slice each into 4 rings. Put water and sugar in a 1-quart glass dish. Heat for 1 minute to dissolve sugar; add lemon juice. Place apple rings in liquid and cook on highest setting for 3 minutes or until apples are soft but not mushy. Place apple rings around the roast and fill the center of each with a prune. Garnish with parsley.

Picture on next page: pork roast with prunes

barbecued spareribs

barbecued spareribs

It is difficult to say exactly how many spareribs to buy because some are more meaty than others. As a rough guide, estimate three-quarters of a pound for each serving, since much of the weight is in the bone. This is a Chinese recipe for barbecue sauce and can also be used for preparing barbecued chicken.

Yield: 2 servings

1½ pounds spareribs, separated into single ribs

68

barbecue sauce

1 clove garlic, finely chopped	1 teaspoon sugar
1½ tablespoons soy sauce	1 teaspoon honey
1½ tablespoons hoisin sauce, or duck sauce	¼ cup chicken broth
1 tablespoon sherry	1 tablespoon oil

Trim the fat from the spareribs and place them in a 9-inch glass baking dish, arranging the meatiest ribs along the sides of the dish. Combine the ingredients for tte barbecue sauce and pour the sauce over the ribs. Let marinate for 2 hours if possible. Turn the ribs after 1 hour.

Cook in the microwave oven on "roast" setting for 30 minutes. Turn the ribs over after 15 minutes and rotate the dish one-quarter of a turn.

pork and orange casserole

pork and orange casserole

This dinner is both nutritious and colorful.

Yield: 4 servings
 3 tablespoons oil
 2 onions, finely chopped
 1½ pounds lean pork, cut into 1½-inch cubes
 ½ cup seasoned flour
 Grated rind and juice of 1 orange
 11-ounce can mandarin oranges
 1 cup water
 1 chicken bouillon cube
 1 green pepper, sliced

Heat the oil in a 2-quart glass or ceramic casserole on the highest setting for 20 seconds. Add the onions and cook for 2 minutes. Add pork coated in seasoned flour. Cook in hot fat for a few seconds to seal in juices. Toss to seal. Grate rind. Squeeze the orange. Drain the mandarin oranges. Mix the syrup from the can with the fresh juice. Combine syrup and juice with water, rind, bouillon cube, and sliced pepper in a small glass or ceramic bowl. Cook on "simmer" setting for 5 minutes. Add to pork. Cover and cook for 20 minutes on "roast" setting. Rotate dish one-quarter of a turn after 10 minutes. Add the mandarin oranges during last 5 minutes. Let stand 10 minutes before serving.

frankfurters with sauerkraut

Other meats, such as cooked pork chops, thickly sliced bacon, or a variety of sausages, including knockwurst, bratwurst, and pork sausages, can also be used to make this dish. Serve with mustard, potatoes baked in their jackets, and a mug of beer.

Yield: 4 servings
 1 pound prepared sauerkraut
 3 slices bacon
 1 teaspoon caraway seeds
 ½ cup white wine
 2 small boiled potatoes, grated
 8 frankfurters
 Freshly ground black pepper

Rinse the sauerkraut in cold water and squeeze dry. Place the bacon slices in a baking dish. Cook for 3 minutes on the highest setting, until crisp. Crumble the bacon and return it to the baking dish. Add all the remaining ingredients. Cover and cook 6 minutes. Rotate the dish a quarter of a turn after 3 minutes.

sweetbreads with orange sauce

The French always blanch sweetbreads before cooking to firm the meat and help keep the pieces whole as it cooks.

Yield: 2 servings

1 sweetbread (about ½ pound)
1 teaspoon salt
2 tablespoons flour
2 tablespoons butter

sauce

½ cup wine vinegar
3 tablespoons confectioner's sugar
1 cup water
¼ teaspoon salt
2 teaspoons cornstarch
Juice of 1 orange
1 teaspoon Grand Marnier liqueur

vegetables

1 large cucumber
1 apple
1 tablespoon butter

In a large bowl add 4 cups water, 6 ice cubes, and sweetbread. Let stand in the refrigerator for 1 hour. In a glass baking dish bring 1 quart of water and 1 teaspoon of salt to a boil on highest setting. Place sweetbread in the water and cook for 1 minute. Remove, and cool in cold water. Remove skin from the sweetbread and cut it lengthwise into equal-size pieces. Salt the slices lightly. Sprinkle with flour, and shake off excess. Melt butter in large baking dish on highest setting for 20 seconds. Add sweetbread slices and cook for 2 minutes on each side.

Peel cucumber and cut in half lengthwise to remove the seeds. With a melon ball spoon, make small balls. Place the cucumbers in a 1-quart glass bowl. Add ¼ cup water, the juice of half a lemon, and a teaspoon of salt. Cook on highest setting for 4 minutes.

Peel apple, cut in half, and remove core. Melt 1 tablespoon of butter in a 1-quart glass bowl on highest setting for 20 seconds. Add apple halves and cook for 1 minute on each side.

To prepare the sauce, in a 2-quart glass casserole combine wine vinegar and confectioner's sugar. Cook on a conventional burner for 5 minutes after syrup starts to boil. (The color of the sauce must be slightly yellow.) Add water and salt and cook in microwave oven for 5 minutes. In a small bowl combine cornstarch and juice of orange. Mix well and pour into the wine vinegar mixture. Stir. Place slices of sweetbreads in this sauce and cook on highest setting 1 minute.

Place slices of sweetbread on serving platter, add Grand Marnier to sauce, stir, and pour over meat slices.

Decorate with apple halves and cucumber balls.

sweetbreads with orange sauce

chinese spareribs with sweet-and-sour sauce

Everybody in the family will enjoy this dinner. Ask the butcher to cut the ribs into small pieces.

Yield: 4 servings

3 pounds spareribs
Freshly ground black pepper
1 teaspoon sugar
1 tablespoon soy sauce
2 tablespoons dry sherry
2 carrots, cut diagonally into 1-inch pieces
1 onion, cut into 1-inch chunks
2 green peppers, cut into 1-inch diamonds
2 tablespoons oil
8 mushroom caps
1 can (8 ounces) pineapple cubes, drained

sweet-and-sour sauce

½ cup sugar
½ cup vinegar
2 tablespoons soy sauce
2 tablespoons dry sherry
3 tablespoons tomato catsup
2 tablespoons cornstarch dissolved in ½ cup pineapple juice

Place the spareribs in a 12-inch glass or ceramic baking dish with the meatiest part to the edges. Add the pepper, sugar, soy sauce, and sherry. Cover with waxed paper and cook on "roast" setting for 30 minutes. Remove from the oven.

Place the carrots, onion, and green peppers in a 1-quart glass or ceramic casserole. Cover with boiling water and cook on the highest setting for 5 minutes. Drain the vegetables.

Heat the ceramic browning plate on the highest setting for 4 minutes. Add the oil. Brown the drained vegetables for 3 minutes. Add the mushroom caps and pineapple cubes and cook 2 minutes. Add the barbecued ribs.

Combine all the ingredients for the sweet-and-sour sauce in a 4-cup glass measuring cup and cook on the highest setting for 2 minutes. Stir and pour over the spareribs. Heat 2 minutes, until very hot. Serve with rice.

pork chops bagatelle

pork chops bagatelle

Stacked or skewered foods can be cooked in a microwave oven if wooden hibachi skewers are used instead of metal skewers.

Yield: 4 servings

8 pork chops
8 slices Gruyère cheese
4 slices ham
2 eggs, beaten
Bread crumbs
¼ cup butter

Stack in sequence and skewer 1 pork chop, 1 slice cheese, ½ slice ham, a second slice of cheese, and another pork chop. Repeat for other 3 skewers. Coat with egg and dip into bread crumbs. Heat butter in a glass baking dish on highest setting for 20 seconds. Add chops and cook on each side for 1 minute. Cover and cook on "roast" setting for 12 to 15 minutes or until pork is thoroughly cooked.

calves liver and bacon

Though it may seem like a startling idea, hot sliced avocados taste marvelous with liver and bacon.

Yield: 4 servings

8 slices bacon
1 tablespoon butter
1 tablespoon oil
4 slices calves liver
1 teaspoon sage
2 tablespoons lemon juice
1 avocado, peeled and sliced
Salt and pepper

Place the bacon on 2 paper plates lined with paper towels. Cook on the highest setting for 3 minutes. Rotate the dish one-quarter of a turn and cook 2 or 3 minutes more, until crisp. Remove the bacon from the oven.

Heat the microwave browning plate on the highest setting for 4 minutes. Add the butter and oil. Place the liver on the plate. Sprinkle with sage and lemon juice. Cook on "simmer" setting for 5 minutes. Rearrange the liver, transferring the pieces from the center to the sides of the plate. Rotate the plate one-quarter of a turn. Place on "roast" setting and cook 4 more minutes. Arrange the avocado slices around the sides of the plate and cook on the same setting for 1½ minutes. Season with salt and pepper. Serve topped with the cooked bacon slices.

marinated rabbit

This is an unusual main dish!

Yield: 4 to 6 servings

1 medium-size rabbit
1 teaspoon salt
¼ teaspoon pepper

marinade

½ bottle red wine
2 cups chicken broth
1 teaspoon allspice
2 bay leaves
1 teaspoon thyme

sauce

½ cup flour for dredging
¼ cup butter
1 dozen pickled white onions (cocktail size)
1 dozen stuffed green olives, sliced
1 pound fresh mushrooms, sliced
2 tablespoons butter

marinated rabbit

Defrost rabbit, if frozen. Rinse and dry. Cut into serving pieces. Rub with salt and pepper and put in a 2-quart bowl. Add the marinade and refrigerate overnight. Drain marinade and reserve. Dry rabbit well and dredge in flour. Heat butter in a 3-quart glass casserole on highest setting for 20 seconds. Add rabbit and cook for 4 minutes. Pour in the marinade, cover, and cook on highest setting for 30 minutes or until tender. Remove from oven.

Melt 2 tablespoons of butter in a 1-quart glass casserole on highest setting for 20 seconds. Add onions, olives, and mushrooms and cook for 3 minutes. Add to the rabbit mixture. Serve with boiled potatoes.

poultry

Cooking Poultry

Chicken, turkey, and other poultry are moist and tender when they are cooked in the microwave oven. To obtain the best results, all poultry that is to be roasted should be trussed with string before cooking. The tips of the wings and the lower parts of the legs can be wrapped loosely with lightweight aluminum foil to prevent them from becoming overcooked. Make sure the foil does not touch the oven walls or there will be "arcing" of the microwaves. Do not salt the skin of poultry before cooking, because salt deflects the pattern of the microwaves and slows down the cooking. However, the cavity of chickens and other birds may be salted.

All poultry to be roasted is cooked breast side down on the highest setting for the first half of the cooking time. The bird is then turned over onto its back and cooked for the remaining time, uncovered, on "roast" setting.

Check the temperature of the cooked poultry immediately after it is taken from the oven. The thermometer should read 175° F. The temperature will rise 20 degrees as the bird stands. Let it rest for 15 minutes after cooking. During this time the cooking will be completed as a result of the transference of its own internal heat.

cooking poultry

Poultry	Cooking Time	Dish	Directions
Capon 5-7 lb	7 min per lb	12-in baking dish	See notes on cooking poultry.
Chicken 2-5 lb	8 min per lb	glass or ceramic 10-in baking dish	See notes on cooking poultry.
Cornish hens 1 hen	12 min	6-in baking dish	
2 hens	24 min	10-in baking dish	
4 hens	36 min	12-in baking dish	Add additional time if additional ingredients are used in recipe.
Duck 5 lb	8 min per lb	12-in baking dish	Set on inverted saucer and remove excess fat as the duck cooks.
Turkey 8-10 lb	6 min per lb	12-in baking dish	
Turkey 10-14 lb	8 min per lb	12-in baking dish	See notes on cooking poultry.

Turkeys weighing over 14 pounds are more successfully cooked in the conventional oven, mainly because the sheer size of the bird is too great for the microwave oven. However, while a large turkey is cooking in the conventional oven, the microwave oven can be making all the accompaniments.

roast chicken royal

This bird is fit for king or consort.

Yield: 4 servings

2½ cups white bread crumbs
1¼ cups milk
1 large egg, beaten
2 medium-size mushrooms, cleaned and chopped
¼ pound ground veal
¼ pound ground pork
½ teaspoon salt
¼ teaspoon pepper
1 4½-pound chicken
2 strips bacon, uncooked
1 clove garlic, minced or crushed
1 tablespoon cooking oil
2 cups chicken broth or bouillon
1 tablespoon cornstarch
1 small jar artichoke hearts
1 8-ounce can mushrooms, drained
1 bunch watercress
1 large orange, cut into wedges

Put bread crumbs and milk in a bowl. Cover and let stand for 30 minutes. Add the beaten egg, chopped mushrooms, veal, and pork. Season well with salt and pepper. Mix to form a firm stuffing.

Dry the chicken skin on paper towels. Season inside with salt and pepper. Put bacon and garlic inside the chicken. Stuff. Truss the chicken and place it breast side down on a microwave oven roasting rack or on an inverted saucer set in a glass baking dish. Brush skin with oil. Cook for 16 minutes on the highest setting. Turn chicken breast side up and rotate pan one-quarter of a turn. Cook on "roast" setting for 16 more minutes, basting frequently with 1 tablespoon oil or drippings from the pan. Transfer chicken to a serving dish and let it rest for 15 minutes before carving.

Strain off all but 2 tablespoons of fat from the roasting pan. Add chicken stock. Stir the cornstarch with 2 tablespoons of cold water and stir into juices in baking dish. Bring to boil on highest setting and cook for 2 minutes or until thick. Stir once after one minute.

In separate glass bowls, heat mushrooms and artichoke hearts in juice from containers. Cook for 2 minutes or until warm. Drain.

Garnish chicken with artichoke hearts, mushrooms, watercress, and orange wedges.

Picture on next page: *(center)*   *(clockwise from top left)*
                            roast chicken royal   *pineapple gateau*
                                                          sole fillets in white wine
                                                          bread sauce
                                                          braised celery

roast chicken

When roasting a chicken in the microwave oven, the cooking time remains the same whether or not it is stuffed. Poultry is best cooked on "roast" setting for half of the cooking time. If it is completely cooked on the highest setting, the meat shrinks from the bone. Allow 8 minutes cooking time per pound.

Yield: 4 servings

1 3½-pound chicken
2 tablespoons butter
Salt and pepper
1 jar (8 ounces) peach preserves
1 tablespoon soy sauce
1 teaspoon powdered ginger
1 teaspoon paprika

Place the butter, salt, and pepper in the chicken cavity. Truss the chicken and place it breast side down on a microwave oven roasting rack or on an inverted saucer set in a glass baking dish. Cook for 14 minutes on the highest setting. Remove from oven. Remove the lid from the jar of preserves and heat on the highest setting for 5 minutes. Force the preserves through a strainer and combine with soy sauce, ginger, and paprika.

Turn the chicken breast side up and brush with the soy sauce mixture. Rotate the chicken one-quarter of a turn. Cook on "roast" setting for 14 more minutes, basting frequently with the soy sauce mixture. Remove the chicken from the oven. The internal temperature should read 175°F. It will increase in temperature 20 degrees as it rests. Let the chicken rest 15 minutes before carving.

a chicken dinner

There are some very attractive round glass baking dishes on the market that are ideal for making this type of arranged dish. The chicken cooks more evenly if the breasts are placed in the center of the dish. This pattern can be followed for making all chicken dishes. Vary the accompanying vegetables as you please. It is especially good served with buttered spinach noodles sprinkled with grated Parmesan cheese. If you are starting with frozen chicken, allow 20 minutes for it to defrost.

Yield: 4 servings

1 3-pound chicken, cut into serving pieces
2 tablespoons oil
1 tablespoon butter
4 leeks, sliced, or 1 onion, finely chopped
2 carrots, sliced
2 stalks celery, sliced
2 tablespoons flour
1 cup chicken broth
½ cup white wine
½ teaspoon marjoram
Salt and pepper

for garnish

1 cup freshly cooked peas and carrots
½ cup sliced mushrooms sautéed in 1 tablespoon butter
2 tablespoons finely chopped parsley

Brown the chicken in a large frying pan in hot combined oil and butter. Remove the chicken and fry the leeks or onion and the carrots and celery for 3 minutes. Stir in the flour and transfer to a glass or ceramic baking dish. Arrange the chicken pieces on top of the vegetables with the breasts in the center of the dish. Add the broth and wine and sprinkle with marjoram. Cook uncovered on "roast" setting for 20 minutes.

Remove from the oven and season with salt and pepper. Arrange the peas, carrots, and mushrooms in the dish and return to the oven. Cook, uncovered, on highest setting for 3 minutes. Garnish with parsley.

chicken breasts with lemon and white vermouth

This is a beautiful and simple recipe. Serve the chicken with rice and spinach or with a tossed salad made from Boston lettuce, sliced raw mushrooms, and an oil-and-lemon-juice dressing.

Yield: 4 servings

8 boneless chicken breasts with skin removed
4 tablespoons butter
4 scallions, finely chopped

Grated rind and juice of 1 lemon
½ teaspoon tarragon or marjoram
⅓ cup white vermouth
Salt and pepper

Arrange the chicken breasts in a 10-inch glass baking dish. Dot with butter and add all the remaining ingredients except the salt and pepper. Cover the chicken with waxed paper. Cook on "roast" setting for 15 minutes. After 7 minutes rearrange the chicken, placing the center pieces at the edge of the dish. Rotate the dish one-quarter of a turn. Season with salt and pepper immediately after the chicken breasts are cooked.

sauce for the chicken breasts

Remove the chicken from the baking dish. Arrange on a bed of steaming hot rice and keep it hot while preparing the sauce.

Yield: 1¼ cups

½ cup whipping cream
1 tablespoon cornstarch dissolved in 2 tablespoons cold water

Salt and pepper
2 tablespoons finely chopped parsley

Pour the cream into the baking dish and cook on the highest setting with the juices from the chicken breasts for 1 minute, until hot. Stir in the cornstarch dissolved in cold water and heat for 1 minute. Stir with a wire whisk. Season with salt and pepper and pour the sauce over the chicken breasts. Garnish with parsley.

barbecued chicken

This sauce can also be used for preparing barbecued spareribs.

Yield: 4 servings

1 3-pound chicken cut into serving pieces

barbecue sauce

½ cup catsup
2 tablespoons chili sauce
1 teaspoon honey or sugar
1 teaspoon mustard

1 tablespoon meat sauce, such as A-1 Sauce or Worcestershire Sauce
1 clove garlic, finely chopped

Place the chicken in a 10-inch glass baking dish. Place the breasts in the center of the dish. Combine the barbecue sauce ingredients and brush the sauce over the surface of the chicken. Cook, uncovered, on "roast" setting for 30 minutes. Turn the chicken pieces over after 15 minutes. Brush with the remaining barbecue sauce and rotate the dish one-quarter of a turn.

chicken with mandarins

Poultry should be completely thawed before cooking. Use a microwave rack.

Yield: 4 to 6 servings

1 5-pound roasting chicken	2 tablespoons butter, melted
2 cups orange juice	1 tablespoon flour
2 tablespoons orange rind	Orange or mandarin segments
⅓ cup brown sugar	for garnish

Combine orange juice, orange rind, sugar, and melted butter. Place chicken in glass baking dish. Sprinkle body cavity with salt and pepper. Truss the chicken with string. Place chicken, breast side down, on microwave roasting rack in a 2-quart glass baking dish. Pour juice mixture over the chicken. Cook on highest setting for 18 minutes. Baste every 15 minutes with pan juices. Turn breast side up and cook on "roast" setting for 18 minutes. Transfer chicken to a hot serving plate and cover with foil for 5 to 10 minutes before serving.

Mix flour with 2 tablespoons cold water and stir into pan drippings with a wire whisk. Bring to a boil on highest setting and cook for 2 minutes or until the sauce has thickened. Stir once after 1 minute. Garnish chicken with orange or mandarin segments and serve with rice or oven-fried potatoes. Serve the sauce separately.

chicken pie

To blend flavors, refrigerate this prior to serving.

Yield: 6 servings

3-pound chicken	2 cups water	10-ounce package frozen peas
1 teaspoon salt	¼ cup butter	3 tablespoons shortening
¼ teaspoon pepper	3½ cups flour	1 small egg, lightly beaten
1 bay leaf	5 tablespoons milk	Slices of cucumber for garnish

Wash chicken; pat dry. Place in a 3-quart glass casserole. Add salt, pepper, bay leaf, and 2 cups of water. Cover and cook on highest setting for 15 minutes. Turn chicken and cook on "simmer" setting for 40 minutes or until chicken is tender. Drain chicken, reserve stock, and cool.

Melt ¼ cup butter in a medium glass bowl on highest setting for 20 seconds. Add ½ cup flour and blend thoroughly. Cook for 2 minutes, stirring twice.

Use 2 cups of broth. Gradually stir into the flour mixture. Heat on highest setting for 2 to 3 minutes, until boiling.

Remove chicken meat from bones and cut up. Mix with sauce and stir in peas. Season with salt and pepper.

Sift rest of flour and a pinch of salt into a mixing bowl. Add remaining margarine and shortening. Cut with two knives or a pastry blender until mixture resembles cornmeal. Add just enough cold water to make a stiff dough. Roll out ⅔ of dough and line an 8-inch baking dish.

Spoon filling into dish. Roll out rest of dough to make a lid for the pie. Put in place. Trim and decorate edge. Reroll trimmings and cut out shapes to decorate top of pie. Brush with beaten egg and bake on "roast" setting for 9 minutes. Transfer to preheated conventional oven at 450°F and bake 10 to 15 minutes or until golden brown.

chicken with mandarins

belgian chicken casserole

In Belgium this casserole, made with chicken and vegetables, is served with chicken soup.

Yield: 4 servings

1 3-pound chicken, cut into serving pieces
Freshly ground black pepper
3 tablespoons butter
4 leeks, sliced, or 2 onions, finely chopped
2 stalks celery, sliced
2 carrots, sliced
2 cups chicken broth
2 egg yolks
2 tablespoons milk or cream
3 tablespoons finely chopped parsley
1 teaspoon salt

Season the chicken with pepper. Heat the butter in a 2½-quart glass or ceramic casserole on the highest setting for 40 seconds. Arrange layers of the vegetables in the casserole and place the chicken pieces on top of the vegetables. Add the chicken broth. Cover and cook on "roast" setting for 30 minutes.

Remove the chicken from the casserole. Discard the skin.

Stir the egg yolks and milk or cream together and add to the casserole. Add the chicken. Cook 2 minutes on the highest setting. Add the parsley and salt. Serve in shallow soup bowls.

sorrento salad

A salad for a summer patio lunch. Serve it with black bread and sweet butter.

Yield: 6 servings

1 3½-pound chicken
1 cup chicken broth
3 tender center stalks celery, chopped
½ red pepper, finely chopped, or 1 jar
    (2 ounces) chopped pimientos
½ cup mayonnaise

¼ cup sour cream
Boston lettuce
2 oranges
1 grapefruit
2 medium-size avocados

Place the chicken in a glass or ceramic casserole just large enough to hold it. Add the chicken broth. Cover and cook on "roast" setting for 25 minutes, until tender. Remove and cool the chicken. Discard the skin and bones and cut the chicken into small pieces. Place the chicken in a bowl with the celery and ¾ of the red pepper or pimiento. Stir together the mayonnaise and sour cream and fold into the chicken mixture.

Line a salad bowl with lettuce leaves. Place the chicken salad in the center of the bowl and garnish with the remaining red pepper. Peel the oranges and grapefruit and cut into segments, cutting between the membranes. Arrange the fruit segments around the chicken salad. Cut and add slices of avocado and intersperse between the fruit at the last minute before serving.

liver paté

This easy paté is perfect with a salad and hunks of French bread.

Yield: 6 or more servings

¼ cup butter
2 medium onions, chopped
1 pound chicken livers
3 tablespoons dry sherry
¼ cup heavy table cream
½ teaspoon garlic salt

¼ teaspoon pepper
1 cup fresh white bread crumbs
2 medium-size eggs
6 strips bacon
Parsley for garnish

Heat butter in a 1-quart glass baking dish on the highest setting for 20 seconds. Add onions and fry for 3 minutes. Add chicken livers, cover with a plate, and cook on "simmer" setting for 8 to 10 minutes or until meat loses its pink color. Put livers and onions in a blender, add sherry and cream, and blend for 1 minute.

Season the liver mixture with garlic salt and pepper. Stir in the bread crumbs, then beat in the eggs until mixture is smooth. Line a 1½-pound glass loaf dish with bacon. Pour the liver mixture into the dish. Cover with plastic wrap. Bake on "simmer" setting for 10 minutes. Cool paté in pan, then unmold. Wrap in foil and store in refrigerator for up to 2 days to blend the flavors. Garnish with a sprig of parsley.

chicken patties

Patties and filling may be made 1 or 2 days in advance. Flavors will blend and taste better.

Yield: 12 patties

1 package 2-crust pie crust mix
2 tablespoons butter
2 teaspoons flour
5 tablespoons milk
½ chicken bouillon cube
¾ cup cooked, diced chicken
2 or 3 tablespoons light cream

Mix pastry according to package directions. Roll out into a rectangle 7 x 10 inches. Cut 12 circles with a 2-inch biscuit cutter. Place on 2 flat-bottomed baking dishes. Mark the patties with a 1-inch biscuit cutter in the center. When baked, this will lift out to give a hollow. Cook one dish at a time on "roast" setting for 7 minutes or until brown spots start to appear on crust.

Melt butter on highest setting for 20 seconds, remove from heat, and stir in the flour. Stir in the milk. Cook for 2 minutes, stirring twice during cooking time. Crumble the bouillon cube into the sauce, and season sauce to taste. Add the chicken and cream. Remove centers from patties, and spoon in filling. Replace small lid if desired.

roast turkey

It is quite difficult to cook a turkey perfectly in the conventional oven because more often than not it becomes dry and tasteless. In the microwave oven it remains moist and full of flavor.

Yield: 6 servings

1 10-pound turkey (there will be enough for sandwiches the next day)
3 tablespoons shortening
1 tablespoon paprika
10 strips bacon

Truss the turkey. Dry the skin with paper towels. Rub the shortening over the skin and sprinkle with paprika. Cover the skin with bacon strips, holding them in place with toothpicks. Cook the turkey, breast side down, uncovered, on a microwave oven roasting rack or on two inverted saucers set in a glass baking dish, for 30 minutes on "roast" setting.

Turn the turkey breast side up. Cover the leg and wing tips with lightweight aluminum foil to prevent them from overcooking. Rotate the turkey one-quarter of a turn and continue cooking for 30 minutes. The internal temperature should read 175°F. It will rise 20 degrees as it rests. Let the turkey rest for 15 minutes before carving.

Note: If you would like to serve stuffing with the turkey, see the recipe for Roast Duck Montmerency.

curried turkey

Brown the turkey well to seal the surface before adding the curry powder. Curry tends to mask the flavor of poultry.

Yield: 6 servings

3 turkey legs and thighs cut at joint into serving pieces
2 tablespoons seasoned flour (add ½ teaspoon salt and ⅛ teaspoon pepper)
2 onions, sliced
¼ cup butter
1 apple, peeled, cored, and chopped
2 tablespoons curry powder
2 cups chicken broth
1 tablespoon lemon juice
2 tablespoons chutney
4 tomatoes, chopped

Coat turkey pieces with seasoned flour. In a conventional oven, fry onions in hot butter until soft. Add turkey and fry until golden brown. Add chopped apple, curry powder, and any remaining flour. Stir well and cook 2 minutes. Add stock, lemon juice, chutney, and tomatoes and mix well. Transfer all ingredients to a large casserole or glass bowl. Cover and cook in microwave oven on "simmer" for about 30 minutes. Cooking time will vary according to the size of turkey pieces. Check for doneness frequently. Serve with rice.

curried turkey

roast turkey with two sauces

These sauces give turkey an unusual and delicious accent.

Yield: 10 servings

1 10-pound turkey	¼ cup Madeira wine
1 teaspoon salt	Oil for basting
½ teaspoon pepper	

Season inside of turkey. Marinate the turkey liver in wine for 15 minutes and return to cavity of bird with 2 tablespoons of the wine. Truss with string. Cook turkey breast side down on microwave roasting rack. Cook on highest setting for 40 minutes, turning turkey once during cooking time. Continue cooking on "roast" setting for 40 minutes, turning turkey once. Serve with sauces.

aphrodisiac sauce

Yield: Sauce for 10

12 small white onions, chopped or thinly sliced
½ cup olive oil
1 tablespoon cinnamon
½ pound raisins (1½ cups)
1½ cups giblet broth (or chicken bouillon)
½ 6-ounce can tomato paste

Heat oil on highest setting for 2 minutes. Carefully add onions, and cook for 5 minutes. Stir at least twice during cooking period. When soft, add the cinnamon, raisins, and broth. Add enough tomato paste to give a sharp taste. Cook on "simmer" setting until well-heated.

metoufe sauce

Yield: Sauce for 10

6 medium-size onions, finely chopped
6 medium-size tomatoes, finely chopped
1 tablespoon parsley, finely chopped
½ cup olive oil
2 tablespoons crushed pimientos

Combine all ingredients, mix thoroughly, and serve.

bread sauce

This sauce is delicious when served with roast poultry.

Yield: 4 servings

1¼ cups milk	¼ teaspoon pepper
1 tablespoon finely grated onion	⅛ teaspoon nutmeg
3 whole cloves	1 tablespoon melted butter
½ teaspoon salt	¾ cup fresh white bread crumbs

Pour milk into a small glass bowl. Add onions and cloves. Bring to a boil on highest setting. Reduce heat to "simmer" setting and cook for 2 minutes. Remove cloves. Season with salt and pepper. Add nutmeg. Add butter and bread crumbs to the milk and blend well. On "simmer" setting, cook until hot.

roast turkey with two sauces

spatchcock turkey

Turkey legs are on sale at various times of the year. They offer excellent food value and a low-cost meal.

Yield: 4 servings

2 turkey legs and thighs, cut at joint into serving pieces
2 teaspoons poultry seasoning
1 teaspoon salt
2 lemons, thinly sliced
¼ cup chutney
1 tablespoon catsup
1 lemon, juiced
¼ cup soft brown sugar
4 whole fresh tomatoes
4 baked or sautéed potatoes

Rub poultry seasoning and salt into turkey. Cover each with lemon slices. In a small glass bowl or casserole combine chutney, catsup, lemon juice, and sugar. On "simmer" setting, heat 1 or 2 minutes, until bubbling. Spoon over turkey joints and cook uncovered on "roast" setting for 20 minutes. Serve with baked tomatoes and baked or sautéed potatoes. Tomato skins must be pierced in several places before cooking in microwave oven. Garnish with lemon slices and parsley.

turkey and cheese cauliflower

It is much easier to remove cooked turkey from the bone while it is still warm—if turkey has cooled, place in colander over hot water until the skin and turkey flesh have softened.

Yield: 4 servings

1 medium-size cauliflower, cut in large florets
Oil and vinegar dressing (mix ⅛ cup oil and ⅛ cup vinegar)
½ cup mayonnaise
¼ cup whipping cream
1 cup cooked turkey, chopped
Salt and pepper
¼ cup grated cheddar cheese

Cook cauliflower. Drain and sprinkle with oil and vinegar dressing. Mix mayonnaise with cream. Add salt and pepper to taste. Add turkey and cauliflower in glass or ceramic bowl; spoon over turkey sauce. Sprinkle with cheese.

Cook for 4 minutes on highest setting. Rotate dish one-quarter turn after 2 minutes. The cheese will not brown in the microwave oven unless you have one of the newer models with the browning element.

spatchcock turkey

turkey and cheese cauliflower

roast duck montmerency

In this recipe the cooking of the duck is completed in the conventional oven so that the skin will crisp and become almost black in color. The duck is served with black cherries.

Yield: 4 servings

1 5-pound duck

stuffing

1 pound sausage meat	3 tablespoons finely chopped parsley
Liver from the duck	1 cup apple sauce
3 slices bread made into bread crumbs in the blender	1 teaspoon cinnamon
½ cup chopped walnuts	1 egg
1 small onion, finely chopped	Salt and pepper

glaze

2 tablespoons honey
2 tablespoons butter, softened

Remove the giblets from the duck and discard excess fat from the duck cavity. The giblets will be used to make the foundation of the sauce for the duck.

Place the sausage meat on a ceramic plate and separate it into small pieces with a fork. Cook the sausage meat for 5 minutes on the highest setting. Chop the duck liver into small pieces and add to the sausage meat. Transfer these ingredients to a bowl. Stir in all the remaining stuffing ingredients and cook in the microwave oven for 3 minutes.

Place the stuffing in the duck cavity and truss the duck with string. Prick the duck skin in several places to allow the fat to drain. Place the duck on an inverted saucer in a 12-inch glass baking dish. Cook the duck on "roast" setting for 20 minutes, rotating the dish one-quarter of a turn after 10 minutes.

Combine the honey and butter and spread over the surface of the duck. Place the duck in a preheated moderate (350°F) oven for 20 minutes to complete the cooking.

Slice the duck meat or cut into quarters with poultry shears.

black cherry garnish for duck

This recipe can also be used for making cherries jubilee.

Yield: 6 servings

1 jar (1 pound) large black Bing cherries
1 tablespoon red currant jelly
1 tablespoon arrowroot or cornstarch dissolved in 2 tablespoons water

Drain the cherries and place in a 4-cup glass measuring cup with 1 cup of the juice. Add the red currant jelly and cook on the highest setting for 3 minutes. Stir in the arrowroot or cornstarch dissolved in cold water and cook for 1 minute until thickened. Stir and serve hot with the duck.

roast duck montmerency

sauce for the duck

This sauce can be made in the microwave oven while the cooking of the duck is completed in a conventional oven.

Yield: 6 servings

1 tablespoon sugar
2 tablespoons red wine vinegar
Giblets from the duck,
    except the liver
½ small onion, finely chopped
1½ cups chicken broth

1 orange
2 tablespoons Grand Marnier
1 tablespoon Madeira or brandy
Salt and pepper
1 tablespoon cornstarch dissolved
    in 2 tablespoons cold water

Place the sugar and red wine vinegar in a custard cup. Cook on the highest setting for 2 minutes, until the sugar has caramelized. Place to one side.

Put the giblets, onion, and chicken broth in a 4-cup glass measuring cup and cook in the microwave oven for 15 minutes at "simmer" setting. Strain ¼ cup of the liquid into the container with the caramelized sugar and return to the measuring cup.

Cut the orange rind into tiny strips, half the length of a matchstick and as thin as possible. Squeeze the orange. Place the orange rind and juice in a custard cup in the microwave oven for 2 minutes on the highest setting. Add to the strained liquid. Add the Grand Marnier, and Madeira or brandy. Season the sauce with salt and pepper. Return to the oven for 2 minutes. Stir in the cornstarch dissolved in cold water and cook 1 minute, until the sauce is thick and bubbling hot.

quail in red wine

Quail and all game birds are difficult to find, but you may be fortunate enough to have your own source of supply. Quail are cooked very successfully in the microwave oven and do not become dry, as is often the case with conventional cooking. If you adapt this recipe for 2 quail, they will be cooked in 20 minutes. The recipe can also be used for 3 Rock Cornish hens. Increase the cooking time by 10 minutes.

Yield: 6 servings

6 quail
6 slices bacon
½ cup red wine
2 tablespoons gin
¾ teaspoon thyme
1 bay leaf
2 tablespoons butter
2 tablespoons flour
1 cup beef broth
2 teaspoons tomato paste
⅓ cup heavy cream
2 tablespoons finely chopped parsley

Remove the giblets from the quail. Cook the bacon on a paper plate, with paper towels, on the highest setting for 5 minutes, until crisp. Remove and crumble the bacon. Truss the quail with string and brown them one at a time in the rendered bacon fat on top of the conventional range. Arrange in a 10-inch glass baking dish. Add the red wine, gin, thyme, and bay leaf. Cover with a piece of waxed paper and cook on "roast" setting for 30 minutes. Rotate the dish one-quarter of a turn and continue cooking on "roast" setting for 20 minutes. Remove the quail and keep them hot.

To prepare the sauce, heat the butter in a 4-cup glass measuring cup on the highest setting for 30 seconds. Stir in the flour. Stir in the strained liquid from the baking dish with a wire whisk. Stir in the beef broth and tomato paste. Add the quail giblets, except for the livers. (The liver makes the sauce cloudy.) Cook for 2 minutes on the same setting, until boiling hot. Add the cream and cook 1 minute. Pour the sauce over the quail and garnish with reserved crumbled bacon and parsley.

Serve on slices of firm-textured bread fried slowly until crisp in equal portions of butter and oil. Fry the bread in a skillet on top of the conventional stove.

seafood

striped bass

All fish are excellent when they are cooked in the microwave oven. In this recipe the fish is topped with fresh vegetables and flavored with a whisper of lemon butter. If you are using frozen fish, allow 10 minutes for it to defrost in your microwave oven.

Yield: 2 servings

1 pound striped bass, cleaned and bones removed
2 scallions, finely chopped
1 small tomato, peeled, seeded, and chopped
½ cup cucumber, diced
¼ teaspoon tarragon or 1 tablespoon chopped parsley
2 tablespoons butter
1 tablespoon lemon juice

Place the bass on a piece of waxed paper large enough to enclose it completely. Top the fish with all the remaining ingredients. Fold the long sides of the paper over the fish and tuck the edges beneath, forming a tidy package. Place on inverted plates and cook for 6 minutes on the highest setting. Rotate the fish one-quarter of a turn after 3 minutes.

braised halibut in cream and white wine

Other firm-textured fish, such as cod, salmon, bass, trout, or swordfish, can also be used for making this dish.

Yield: 6 servings

3 pounds halibut
4 scallions, finely chopped
2 carrots, thinly sliced
2 stalks celery, thinly sliced
½ teaspoon thyme
Grated rind of 1 lemon
2 tablespoons butter
½ cup cream
½ cup white wine
1½ tablespoons flour
Salt and pepper
2 tablespoons freshly chopped parsley

Place the fish in a 10-inch glass or ceramic baking dish. Arrange the vegetables around the sides of the dish. Sprinkle the fish with thyme and grated lemon rind. Dot with 1 tablespoon of the butter. Pour in the cream and wine. Cover with waxed paper and cook on "roast" setting for 12 minutes. Rotate the dish one-quarter of a turn after 6 minutes. Transfer the fish to a hot platter and season with salt and pepper. Allow to stand for 5 minutes. It should flake easily, indicating it is completely cooked.

Heat the remaining 1 tablespoon of butter in a 6-cup glass measuring cup on the highest setting for 20 seconds and then stir into the vegetables and liquid in the baking dish. Cook for 5 minutes on the same setting. Spoon the sauce over the fish and garnish with parsley.

"broiled" salmon

This is an almost-instant dinner and is in itself worthy of the cost of the microwave oven. On a self-indulgent evening serve yourself the salmon with mock Hollandaise sauce, a boiled butter-drenched potato, and a mouthful of peas.

Yield: 1 serving

2 tablespoons butter	Sprig of parsley
1 6-ounce salmon steak	Salt and pepper
2 teaspoons lemon juice	

Preheat a ceramic browning plate for 3 minutes. Add half of the butter. Place the salmon on the buttered plate and dot the surface with the remaining butter. Sprinkle with lemon juice and add the parsley sprig. Cook for 2 minutes on the highest setting. Rotate the dish one-quarter of a turn and cook for another 2 minutes. Season with salt and pepper.

Note: If you are cooking two salmon steaks, cook them 3 minutes on the first side and 2 minutes on the second side.

mock hollandaise sauce

The microwave oven cooks food with such fantastic speed that it is almost impossible to make a true Hollandaise sauce in it. Instead, however, you can make an extremely good version. The mayonnaise in this recipe stabilizes the egg yolks.

Yield: 4 servings

8 tablespoons butter	¼ cup mayonnaise
3 egg yolks	Salt and pepper
2 tablespoons lemon juice	Dash cayenne pepper

Cut the butter into small pieces and heat in a 4-cup glass measuring cup on the highest setting for 50 seconds, until hot and bubbling. Stir in the egg yolks, lemon juice, and mayonnaise, stirring rapidly with a small wire whisk. Return to the oven for 50 seconds. Stir rapidly after 25 seconds and immediately after it is taken from the oven. Season with salt, pepper, and cayenne.

salmon in pastry
Yield: 4 servings

1 tablespoon butter	¼ teaspoon white pepper
2 tablespoons flour	1 tablespoon chopped parsley
¾ cup milk	2 eggs, hard-boiled, shelled,
1 small can salmon	and chopped
½ teaspoon salt	1 crust pie pastry, uncooked

Place butter, flour, and milk in a small pan. Bring to a boil on conventional burner, whisking constantly. Cook for 2 minutes.

Drain salmon; remove skin and bones. Stir salmon and remaining ingredients into sauce. Roll out pastry to a 10-inch square and place in a glass baking dish. Place filling in center. Brush pastry edges with water. Fold corners to center and pinch edges together so that the filling is completely enclosed. Brush with a little milk and cook on "roast" setting for 9 minutes or until crust has small brown spots.

fillets of sole with vegetables

Fish is done when it is white and opaque. Separate the flakes near the center with a fork to test that it is fully cooked.

Yield: 2 servings

2 fillets of sole (about 1 pound)
¾ cup heavy cream
1 stalk celery, thinly sliced
1 scallion, thinly sliced
2 carrots, thinly sliced
½ teaspoon salt
1 tablespoon butter

Melt the 1 tablespoon of butter in a medium baking dish for 20 seconds on the highest setting. Add vegetable slices and salt. Cook for 2 minutes. While stirring rapidly, add the cream. Cook for 3 minutes. Add in the sole and cook 3 minutes. Remove fillets of sole and set on serving plate. Cook sauce 1 additional minute. Take out of oven. Pour sauce over slices of sole.

fillets of sole with tomatoes

The wine used for poaching the sole becomes a delicious sauce enriched with cream.

Yield: 8 servings

3 pounds fillets of sole
¼ pound butter
1 large onion, finely chopped
3 scallions
3 sprigs parsley
½ cup chopped watercress
2 large tomatoes, peeled, seeded, and chopped
½ teaspoon tarragon
½ teaspoon salt
⅛ teaspoon pepper
1 cup dry white wine
1 egg yolk, beaten
¾ cup heavy cream
1 tablespoon lemon juice

fillets of sole with tomatoes

In a large glass baking dish add butter, onion, scallions, watercress, tomatoes, and tarragon. Add the sole to the dish. Add salt, pepper, and wine. Cover and cook on highest setting for 12 minutes. Let stand, covered, for 5 minutes. Remove the fillets and keep them warm. Continue to cook the sauce until the volume is reduced by one-third. Remove from microwave oven and rapidly stir in the egg yolk and the cream. Taste and adjust seasoning as desired. Add lemon juice. Return the fillets to the cooking dish and spoon the sauce over them. Broil in a conventional broiler on low heat for 5 minutes to brown.

fillets of sole with vegetables

rolled fillets of sole

If you have a food processor, the preparation time of this elegant dish is greatly reduced. A splendid dinner, this could well become a specialty of your house.

Yield: 6 servings

3½ pounds fillets of sole
4 tablespoons butter
½ pound fresh mushrooms, chopped very finely
4 scallions, chopped very finely
3 tablespoons finely chopped parsley
Dash cayenne pepper
3 tablespoons flour
½ cup heavy cream
1 tablespoon lemon juice
½ cup cooked shrimp or lobster, chopped very finely
Salt and pepper
1 cup white wine
Chopped pimiento

Cut each fish fillet in half lengthwise. Allow 2 half fillets for each serving. Pound the remaining raw fish to form a purée and place to one side.

Heat the butter in a glass or ceramic casserole on the highest setting for 30 seconds. Add the mushrooms and scallions and cook for 2 minutes. Stir after 1 minute. Stir in the parsley, cayenne pepper, and flour. Add the cream and lemon juice, stirring rapidly with a wire whisk to prevent curdling. Cook 3 minutes. Stir in the pounded sole and cook 1 minute. Stir in the shrimp or lobster. The mixture will be very thick. Taste and season with salt and pepper.

Place a little of the mushroom mixture (reserving the remainder for the sauce) at the wide end of each fish fillet half, and roll the fillets. Secure with toothpicks. Arrange the fillets in a 14-inch glass or ceramic baking dish. Add the white wine. Cover and cook on the highest setting for 8 minutes. Rotate the dish one-quarter of a turn after 4 minutes. Reserve the wine cooking liquid for the sauce and transfer the fish to a hot serving plate. Garnish with chopped pimiento.

sauce for rolled fillets of sole

2 tablespoons butter
2 tablespoons flour
Reserved cooking wine from the fish
½ cup chicken broth
1 small tomato, peeled, seeded, and chopped
1 teaspoon tomato paste
Reserved extra mushroom mixture
¼ cup tiny Icelandic shrimp, canned or fresh

Heat the butter in a 4-cup glass measuring cup for 30 seconds on the highest setting. Stir in the flour and cook for 50 seconds. Stir in the reserved wine and add chicken broth. Stir with a wire whisk. Add the chopped tomato and tomato paste. Cook 3 minutes. Stir in the reserved mushroom mixture and cook 2 minutes. Stir in the shrimp. Serve the sauce separately.

sole fillets in white wine

The shrimps lend a new and delicious taste to the fish.

Yield: 4 servings

2 large sole fillets,
   (ask for fish bones)
1 cup water
1 teaspoon salt
¼ teaspoon pepper
1 bay leaf
1 small carrot, sliced
½ small onion, sliced
5 tablespoons milk
½ cup flour

¼ cup butter
1 cup shelled shrimps, uncooked
   and chopped
Cayenne pepper, to taste
3 tablespoons grated Parmesan cheese
½ cup dry white wine
½ small green pepper, for garnish
1 small lemon, sliced, for garnish
Few sprigs of parsley, for garnish

Place the fish bones in a 2-quart glass bowl or casserole with water. Add salt, pepper, bay leaf, carrot, and onion. On highest setting, bring to a boil. Reduce heat to "simmer" setting and cook for 10 minutes. Strain stock and cool.

Combine milk and flour in a medium bowl and blend to a smooth paste. Stir in fish stock. Cook on "simmer" setting for 3 minutes, stirring twice. Remove from heat. Stir in 2 tablespoons butter and shrimp. Add a dash of cayenne pepper to taste. Stir in 2 tablespoons cheese. Roll fillets and stand them in a buttered baking dish. Ease open the middle of each fillet to make a 1-inch hole. Secure rolls with a toothpick. Fill the fillets with sauce. Cover and cook on highest setting for 8 to 9 minutes. Sprinkle the remaining cheese on fish, and re-cover. Let fish stand, covered, for 5 minutes to complete cooking.

Strain fish juices from baking dish into a medium glass bowl. Add 2 tablespoons butter and the white wine. Bring to a boil on highest setting and continue to boil until mixture is reduced by half. Pour into a sauce boat. Serve the fish on a bed of cooked rice mixed with sliced green pepper. Garnish with lemon twists and parsley.

anchovy fingers

These may be made the day before and served hot or cold.

Yield: Depends on amount of pastry trimmings

Pie pastry trimmings
Anchovies soaked in milk
2 tablespoons grated cheddar cheese

Soak fillets in milk for half an hour to remove excess salt. Place pastry trimmings on top of the other in a neat stack and then roll to a rectangle about ¼ inch thick. Sprinkle the grated cheese on the dough and cut into fingers ¾ x 2½ inches. Place the fingers on a flat baking dish and place an anchovy fillet on each. Cook on "roast" setting for 7 to 9 minutes. If a brown color is desired, cook in a conventional oven at 450°F for a few minutes.

trout in lemon aspic

Here is a splendid, sophisticated summer supper to serve with a tossed salad and tiny new potatoes. If you do not have a serving platter large enough to hold 4 trout, use separate serving plates.

Yield: 4 servings

4 whole fresh lake trout, each weighing
  approximately 8 ounces
1½ cups white wine
1 cup chicken consommé
3 tablespoons lemon juice
2 tablespoons dry sherry
1 small onion, cut into rings
3 sprigs parsley
½ cup chopped parsley
1½ envelopes unflavored gelatin
Salt
1 lemon, thinly sliced and seeds removed

Place the trout in a 12-inch glass or ceramic baking dish. Add the white wine, chicken consommé, lemon juice, sherry, onion, and parsley sprigs. Cover with waxed paper and cook for 8 minutes on "simmer" setting until the fish flakes easily. (The liquid should simmer, not boil.) Take the trout from the baking dish and remove the skin carefully. Place to one side.

Discard the parsley sprigs and all but 8 onion rings. Stir the chopped parsley and gelatin into the hot broth. Let stand for 3 minutes. Return the broth to the microwave oven and cook, uncovered, on the highest setting for 2 minutes, until hot but not boiling.

Pour the lemon aspic into a serving dish with a shallow rim and allow to cool slightly. Arrange the fish attractively in the serving dish before the aspic has set. Place 2 onion rings on top of each trout. Arrange the lemon slices in the dish, and spoon the aspic over all. Chill for 4 hours before serving with the following sauce.

sauce for trout and other seafood

Yield: 4 servings

1 cup mayonnaise
½ cup sour cream
1 teaspoon Dijon mustard
2 tablespoons tomato catsup
1 hard-boiled egg, finely chopped
1 jar (2 ounces) chopped pimientos
2 tablespoons chopped chives
2 teaspoons capers (optional)

Stir together the mayonnaise, sour cream, mustard, catsup, and hard-boiled eggs. Combine the pimientos, chives, and capers, and arrange on top of the flavored mayonnaise. Stir the sauce ingredients together at the table so that the colors will remain bright.

swordfish with white wine

Swordfish makes a very satisfying dinner when you are really hungry. However, when it is broiled, it tends to become rather dry and somewhat tasteless. It is at its best when it is cooked in the microwave oven.

Yield: 4 servings

2 pounds swordfish
½ cup dry white wine
1 tablespoon lemon juice
4 scallions, finely chopped
3 tablespoons finely chopped parsley
2 tablespoons butter
Salt and pepper

Remove the skin from the swordfish and place in a baking dish just large enough to accommodate it. Pour the wine and lemon juice over the fish. Sprinkle the surface with scallions and parsley. Dot with butter and season with pepper.

Cover with waxed paper and cook on "roast" setting for 12 minutes. Rotate the dish one-quarter of a turn every 3 minutes. Remove from the oven and season with salt. Let stand 5 minutes before serving.

bouillabaisse

A recipe from Provence, this feast of fish is delicately flavored with saffron, orange rind, and Pernod.

Yield: 6 servings

2½ pounds assorted firm-textured white fish
    such as sea bass, halibut, cod, or jumbo shrimp
1 pound fish trimmings, skins, bones, and heads
3 leeks, sliced, or 1 onion, chopped
4 cloves garlic, crushed
3 sprigs parsley
1 teaspoon thyme
1 bay leaf
¼ teaspoon saffron
Grated rind of 2 oranges
½ cup Pernod
1½ cups white wine
2 tomatoes, peeled, seeded, and chopped

Remove the skin and bones from the fish and cut into 1½-inch cubes. Place to one side.

Place the fish trimmings in a 3-quart glass or ceramic casserole with the leeks or onion, garlic, parsley, thyme, and bay leaf. Add 6 cups of water. Cover and cook on the highest setting for 10 minutes. Strain the liquid and return to the casserole. Add the saffron, grated orange rind, Pernod, and white wine. Add the fish, cover, and cook 6 minutes. Add the tomatoes and cook 3 minutes. Serve hot in soup bowls with garlic bread.

haddock with tomato sauce

This quickly prepared meal must be made with the freshest of fish and the ripest of summer tomatoes. If frozen fish and canned tomatoes are used, it may look similar, but it will be a mere hint of its potential delight.

Yield: 4 servings

2 pounds haddock
2 tablespoons butter

tomato sauce

4 medium-size tomatoes,
  cut into wedges
1 onion, finely chopped
2 tablespoons white vermouth
1 tablespoon olive oil

1 teaspoon flour
2 teaspoons tomato paste
½ teaspoon thyme
½ teaspoon basil
Salt and pepper

Dot the haddock with butter. Wrap it in waxed paper. Place it in a 10-inch glass or ceramic baking dish and cook on the highest setting for 6 minutes. Rotate the dish one-quarter of a turn after 3 minutes.

To prepare the sauce, place all the ingredients in a glass or ceramic casserole. Cover and cook on the highest setting for 8 minutes. Purée the sauce in a blender and strain to remove the tomato skins and seeds. Reheat the sauce, uncovered, for 3 minutes and serve with the fish.

seafood rissoto

Yield: 4 servings

2 cups uncooked rice
1 small onion, chopped
¼ cup butter
½ pound medium shrimp
¼ pound mushrooms
1 stalk celery, chopped
1 red pepper, sliced
1 package frozen green peas
¼ teaspoon saffron

2 tablespoons finely chopped parsley
¼ cup grated Parmesan cheese
2 small onions, sliced
½ stalk celery
1 clove garlic
1 cup white wine
½ teaspoon salt
¼ teaspoon pepper

Peel and devein shrimp. Put stock ingredients plus shrimp peels and 2½ cups water in a 1½-quart glass or ceramic casserole. Cook at highest setting for 5 minutes. Strain.

Melt butter in a 2½-quart casserole for 20 seconds. Add onion and cook for 2 minutes, until transparent. Add rice and stir well. Pour in strained stock. Cook for 12 minutes. Rotate the dish one-quarter turn every 2 minutes. Add celery, red pepper, thawed peas, mushrooms, shrimp, and ground saffron. Cover casserole and cook 6 minutes on highest setting, until shrimp are pink. Stir mixture and rotate the dish one-quarter of a turn after 3 minutes. Before serving, sprinkle with parsley and grated Parmesan cheese.

seafood rissoto

seafood quiche lorraine

Use the lowest setting for this custard dish.

Yield: 6 servings

pastry

1¼ cups flour
6 tablespoons butter
3 tablespoons cold water
3 tablespoons light cream

cheese filling

3 eggs
1¼ cups grated Gruyère cheese
¼ cup grated Parmesan cheese
¾ cup milk
½ cup light cream
¼ teaspoon paprika or white pepper
⅛ teaspoon nutmeg
½ teaspoon salt
For shellfish choose among: 4 ounces shrimp, crab, or lobster

pastry

Sift flour into a bowl. Cut in butter with a knife or pastry blender until mixture looks mealy. Make a hole in the center and pour the water and cream into it. Work the pastry with a spoon until it can be formed into a ball. Chill thoroughly. Roll out to fit an 8- or 9-inch glass pie plate. Flute edge; prick bottom and sides of crust with fork. Cook on "roast" setting for 7 minutes.

cheese and seafood filling

Beat the eggs. Add cheeses, milk, cream, seasonings, and spices. Arrange the shellfish, cleaned and shelled, in the pie shell. Pour the cream mixture into the pie shell and cook on "defrost" setting for 30 to 35 minutes or until a knife inserted in the center comes out clean. Let quiche stand 5 minutes before serving.

seafood quiche lorraine

fish bonne femme in crepes

Although this recipe involves several steps, the total time is less than 1 hour for a delectable main dish.

Yield: 4 servings

batter

> ½ cup flour
> Pinch salt
> 1 egg
> 5 tablespoons milk

filling

> 1 pound white fish (sole, haddock, etc.) fillets
> ¼ cup butter
> Salt and pepper
> 2 tablespoons water
> ¼ cup white wine
> ½ pound mushrooms
> 1 tablespoon onion, finely chopped

sauce

> 3 tablespoons butter
> 4 tablespoons flour
> 1¼ cups milk

garnish

> Pastry crescents

Combine batter ingredients and beat to blend. Make 8 very thin crepes in the usual way. Heat half the butter in a 2-quart glass or ceramic casserole on the highest setting for 20 seconds. Add fish and cook each side for 1 minute. Sprinkle with salt and pepper, then pour the water and wine into the casserole. Cover with waxed paper and cook for 6 minutes on "simmer" setting until the fish flakes easily. While fish is cooking, slice mushrooms. Remove fish from oven and keep it warm. Heat remainder of butter in a medium glass bowl on the highest setting for 20 seconds. Stir in mushrooms and onion and cook for 2 minutes. Pour onto center of a heated serving dish and keep it warm. Fold 2 sides of each crepe into the middle to form cone shapes. Remove fish from the liquid (reserve this for sauce) and place a piece of fish in each crepe. Fold over to form a roll. Place the rolls on top of the mushroom mixture. Keep warm.

For the sauce: Melt butter in a small pan on conventional burner; stir in flour. Cook slowly to brown; gradually add milk and cook, stirring constantly, until thick. Add liquid from the fish and extra seasoning to taste, if necessary. Pour over rewarmed crepes and garnish with crescents of cooked pie pastry. (This is a useful way of using leftover pastry. The crescent can be stored in a tight container and reheated before using as a garnish.)

fish bonne femme in crepes

baked cod

Other fish, such as haddock or rockfish, could be substituted for the cod in this recipe.

Yield: 4 servings

1 dressed fresh cod, about 2 pounds
4 tomatoes, sliced
3 lemons
1 pound mushrooms
½ teaspoon salt
⅛ teaspoon pepper
½ teaspoon marjoram
½ teaspoon thyme
1 bay leaf
1 large onion
3 tablespoons cooking oil

Wash fish, pat dry, and place in a medium glass baking dish. Sprinkle the juice of 1 lemon over the fish. Garnish with the tomatoes and remaining lemons cut into slices. Wash the mushrooms and place around the fish. Season with salt and pepper. Add marjoram, thyme, and bay leaf. Cut the onions into rings and add. Sprinkle with cooking oil. Cook covered on highest setting for 14 minutes. Let fish stand, covered, for 5 minutes. *Picture on previous page: baked cod*

baked rockfish

baked rockfish

Cucumbers make an unusual garnish for this fish entree.

Yield: 8 servings

    1 dressed rockfish with head, approximately 4 pounds
    2 tomatoes, cored, peeled, and seeded
    1 pound mushrooms
    6 scallions
    1 small clove garlic, minced
    ½ teaspoon thyme
    1 bay leaf
    2 tablespoons finely chopped parsley
    ½ teaspoon salt
    ½ teaspoon pepper
    2 cups dry white wine
    6 tablespoons butter
    ½ lemon

Grease a large glass baking dish. Wash the fish, pat dry, and place in the dish. Slice tomatoes, mushrooms, and scallions, and place them around fish. Add garlic, thyme, bay leaf, parsley, salt, and pepper. Cover with wine and dot with 4 tablespoons of butter, cut into small pieces. Tuck waxed paper over dish to cover. Cook on highest setting for 18 minutes. Let stand, covered, for 5 minutes. Remove fish and place on a serving dish.

Soften (but do not melt) 2 tablespoons of butter. Strain and pour off juice from the baking dish and whip soft butter into it until the mixture is light. Add the cooked vegetables to the sauce. Taste and add additional seasoning if necessary. Add the juice of ½ lemon and serve with the fish.

Idea for vegetable: Cut 2 medium-size cucumbers into quarters, place in a cheesecloth bag, and immerse in salted boiling water for 5 minutes. Immediately after boiling, butter the hot sections and sprinkle with chopped parsley. Arrange around the fish with sections of lemon and sprigs of parsley. Serve immediately.

curried shrimp

Curries can range from very simple to highly elaborate dishes, and much of the pleasure of eating a good curry is the variety of the accompaniments.

Yield: 4 servings

1½ pounds medium-size fresh shrimp	**Dash cayenne pepper**
2 tablespoons oil	**2 tablespoons flour**
1 onion, finely chopped	**1½ cups chicken broth**
½ green pepper, finely chopped	**1 teaspoon lemon juice**
1 tablespoon curry powder	**1 tablespoon tomato paste**
¼ teaspoon cumin	

Peel and devein the shrimp and leave to one side.

Heat the oil in a 1½-quart glass or ceramic casserole on the highest setting for 30 seconds. Add the onion and green pepper and cook for 1 minute. Stir in the curry powder, cumin, and cayenne pepper. Cook for 20 seconds. Stir in the flour. Stir in the chicken broth, lemon juice, and tomato paste with a wire whisk. Cook for 3 minutes. Add the shrimp and cook 3 minutes.

Serve with rice and chutney. Sprinkle with toasted coconut.

Note: For a touch of drama, the curried shrimp can be served inside a hollowed pineapple shell. Scoop out the shell carefully and cut the pineapple into small cubes. Heat the pineapple in its juice, uncovered, in the microwave oven for 4 minutes. Drain and serve hot in a separate bowl.

toasted coconut

Spread 1 cup grated coconut on a paper plate and cook, uncovered, on the highest setting for 2 minutes. Stir the coconut and cook for 1 minute more. Sprinkle part of the coconut over the shrimp and serve the remainder in a separate bowl.

vegetables

Cooking Vegetables

All vegetables are cooked in covered dishes, in freezer cartons, or in plastic pouches. All are rotated one-quarter of a turn halfway through the cooking period. Salt can be added to vegetables if they are cooked in water. If they are cooked in cartons, add salt after the cooking is completed. All fresh vegetables are cooked in one-third to one-half of the conventional cooking time. Canned vegetables are cooked in the liquid in which they are canned and need only be reheated. A 1-pound can of vegetables is hot in 3 minutes. Transfer the vegetables to a 1-quart glass or ceramic casserole for reheating.

To cook vegetables frozen in cartons, remove the outer wrappings or the dye may stain the bottom of the oven. Open the carton at one end. Place icy side up and allow roughly 5 minutes cooking time on the highest setting. Err on the side of undercooking rather than overcooking, because more time can always be added, but overcooked vegetables are one of life's few avoidable disasters. Remember, too, that the vegetables continue to cook for a minute or two after they are removed from the oven.

Many frozen vegetables that are prepared in butter and packed in pouches have recommended times for microwave oven cooking printed on the box. All these times can be trusted. Cut a slit in the pouch before cooking, as the steam pressure may build so greatly within the package as to cause it to burst.

Most satisfactory results are obtained when cooking one pound or less of a vegetable. Larger quantities require a longer cooking time and are more successfully cooked on top of the stove.

cooking vegetables

Food	Quantity	Directions	Time
Artichoke (fresh)	1	Cover with cold water.	6 min after water reaches boiling point. Add 2 min additional time for each additional artichoke.
Artichoke hearts (frozen)	10-oz pkg	Add ¼ cup water.	4 min
Asparagus spears (fresh, medium thickness)	1 lb	Add ½ cup water.	6 min
Asparagus (frozen)	10-oz pkg	Add ¼ cup water.	6 min
Beans, string Wax Green (fresh)	1 lb	Add ½ cup water.	6 min
(frozen)	10-oz pkg	Add ¼ cup water.	7 min Add 2 min additional time for lima beans.
Broccoli (fresh)	1 lb	Add ½ cup water. Arrange florets to the center of the dish.	6 min
(frozen)	10-oz pkg	Add ¼ cup water.	6 min
Brussels sprouts (fresh)	1 lb	Add ½ cup water.	8 min
(frozen)	10-oz pkg	Add ¼ cup water.	7 min
Cabbage	3 cups	Add ½ cup water.	6 min
Carrots (fresh) sliced	4 medium	Add ½ cup water.	6 min
(frozen)	10-oz pkg	Add ¼ cup water.	5 min
Cauliflower florets (fresh)	1 medium head	Add ½ cup water.	8 min

(frozen)	10-oz pkg	Add ¼ cup water.	7 min
Corn on the cob (fresh)	2 ears	Butter generously. Cover with waxed paper. Place on a plate.	3 min
(frozen)	2 ears	Same	3 min
Corn kernels (frozen)	10-oz pkg	Add 2 tbs water.	3 min
Onion, chopped or sliced (fresh)	1 medium size	Cook in 2 tbs melted butter.	2 min
Potatoes baked	1	Pierce with ice pick or fork in 4 places. Place on paper plate. Cover with waxed paper.	4 min
	2	Same	6 min
	4	Same	8 min
roast	2	Place on ceramic plate with 2 tbs oil.	4 min
boiled	4 medium size	Cover with water.	Cook 4 min after water reaches boiling point.
Potatoes (sweet)	1	Pierce as above.	3½ min
	2	Same	7 min
	4	Same	14 min
Spinach (fresh)	1 lb	No added water.	3 min
(frozen)	10-oz pkg	Add 2 tbs water.	4 min
Squash acorn butternut	1 medium	Cut in half. Remove seeds. Add 2 tbs butter. Place on plate. Cover with waxed paper.	8 min
Zucchini sliced	1 lb	Add 1 tbs butter.	3 min

asparagus and cottage cheese salad

This salad, made when the first tender asparagus appears in the springtime, can be served alone or with rolled slices of boiled Virginia ham.

Yield: 6 servings

1½ pounds thin asparagus spears	1 pound cottage cheese
½ teaspoon salt	1 cup sour cream
Freshly ground black pepper	3 tablespoons chopped chives
2 tablespoons lemon juice	Pimiento strips
6 tablespoons olive oil	

Wash the asparagus in plenty of cold water to remove any sand. Cut the spears into uniform lengths. Peel the lower third of each spear with a potato peeler. Arrange in a 10-inch glass or ceramic flat baking dish with the tips in the center of the dish. Sprinkle with salt and add cold water to cover. Cook, covered, on the highest setting until the water reaches the boiling point. Rotate the dish one-quarter of a turn and cook for 3 more minutes. Taste a spear to be sure it is tender but slightly crisp. Drain and rinse immediately but briefly under cold running water. Return the asparagus to the baking dish.

Combine the salt, pepper, lemon juice, and oil, and pour over the warm asparagus. Let stand for 5 minutes and drain off the dressing.

Arrange the asparagus on a flat serving plate with the tips pointing to the edge of the plate. Combine the cottage cheese and sour cream and place in the center of the dish. Sprinkle with chopped chives and garnish with pimiento strips.

asparagus with white sauce

When asparagus is in season, it can be served in many delectable ways. This method is beautiful with roast chicken or ham.

Yield: 6 servings

2 pounds uniform-size fresh asparagus spears	1 tablespoon lemon juice
½ cup cold water	1 teaspoon salt
	1 tablespoon butter

white sauce

2 tablespoons butter	⅛ teaspoon nutmeg
2 tablespoons flour	Salt and pepper
¾ cup milk	2 hard-boiled eggs
¾ cup light cream	

Trim the asparagus (see recipe for Asparagus and Cottage Cheese Salad) and place in a baking dish. Add the water, lemon juice, and salt. Cover with waxed paper and cook on the highest setting for 6 minutes. Drain and immediately rinse under cold running water. Place on a serving dish, dot with butter, and keep the asparagus warm while preparing the sauce.

Heat the butter in a 4-cup measuring glass for 30 seconds on the highest setting. Stir in the flour, milk, cream, nutmeg, salt, and pepper, and cook for 3 minutes. Stir with a wire whisk twice to ensure a smooth sauce. Reserve 1 egg yolk. Chop the remaining yolk and whites and add to the hot sauce. Place the sauce in a sauce boat and sprinkle with the remaining chopped egg yolk. Reheat the asparagus for 1½ minutes just before serving with the sauce.

asparagus with white sauce

mushrooms with cheese sauce

Chops or plain roasted meats are good served with a sauced vegetable. This dish is completed in the conventional oven.

Yield: 4 servings

8 large mushrooms
3 slices bacon
1 tablespoon butter
4 scallions, finely chopped
1 clove garlic, finely chopped

2 tablespoons flour
1¼ cups milk
¼ cup grated Swiss cheese
½ cup bread crumbs
¼ cup grated Parmesan cheese

Remove the stems from the mushrooms and chop them finely. Fry the bacon in an 8-inch glass baking dish on the highest setting for 3 minutes, until the fat is rendered. Remove and crumble the bacon. Add the butter to the bacon fat and brown the mushroom caps for 1½ minutes. Remove the mushroom caps and fry the chopped stems, scallions, and garlic for 1½ minutes. Stir in the flour and cook 30 seconds. Stir in the milk and cook 2 minutes. Stir in the grated Swiss cheese. Cook 50 seconds. Return the mushroom caps and crumbled bacon to the baking dish. Top with bread crumbs and grated Parmesan cheese. Place under a preheated broiler for 3 minutes. The crumbs will not brown in the microwave oven unless you have one of the newest models with the browning attachment.

onions in beef broth and red wine

An accompaniment for roast beef: Tiny white onions are browned in butter, glazed, and served in a good rich sauce. A cross is cut at the root end of each onion to prevent the inside from falling out of the onion.

Yield: 8 servings

1½ pounds small white onions, peeled, with a cross cut in the root ends
1 cup beef broth
1 cup red wine
1 tablespoon tomato paste
¼ teaspoon thyme
½ teaspoon salt
1 tablespoon oil
1 tablespoon butter
1 tablespoon sugar
2 tablespoons flour

Heat microwave browning plate for 4 minutes. Add the oil and butter and brown the onions on the highest setting for 4 minutes. Sprinkle with sugar. Stir the onions and cook for 1½ minutes. Transfer to a 1½-quart glass or ceramic casserole. Stir the flour into the onions and add all the remaining ingredients. Cover and cook for 10 minutes until the onions are tender.

Note: As you will see in the vegetable-timing chart, 1 pound of whole white onions is cooked in 5 minutes. However, additional time must be added for cooking 1½ pounds of onions as well as the extra time required for heating the wine and broth to the boiling point.

stuffed cabbage leaves

Stuffed cabbage has all the virtues of taste and economy. Allow 2 stuffed cabbage leaves for each serving and then 1 or 2 extra.

Yield: 6 servings

1 medium-size cabbage
1 tablespoon oil
1 onion, finely chopped
1 pound ground chuck steak
1½ cups cooked rice
1 tablespoon tomato paste
¼ cup finely chopped parsley
¼ teaspoon allspice
½ teaspoon cinnamon
1 teaspoon salt
Freshly ground black pepper
½ cup beef broth
1 cup tomato sauce

Place the cabbage in a 3-quart glass or ceramic casserole. Add ½ cup cold water, cover, and cook 4 minutes on the highest setting, until the leaves can be loosened easily. Discard the tough outer leaves and select 12 or 14 large perfect leaves. Remove the heavy stems. (Use the remaining cabbage for another meal.)

Heat the oil in a 2-quart glass bowl in the microwave oven for 20 seconds. Add the onion and cook 1 minute on the highest setting. Add the ground beef and cook for 3 minutes. Break up the beef with a fork and rotate the dish one-quarter of a turn after 1½ minutes. Combine the onion and beef with the rice, tomato paste, parsley, allspice, cinnamon, salt, and pepper.

Place a little of the mixture in the center of each leaf. Fold the sides over and roll the leaves to form tidy packages. Place seam side down in a 12-inch glass baking dish. Add the beef broth and tomato sauce. Cover with waxed paper and cook for 8 minutes on the highest setting. Rotate the dish one-quarter of a turn after 3 minutes.

spinach tarts

Make pastry 3 or 4 days in advance and store in a plastic bag.

Yield: 6 to 8 servings

1½ cups flour
Pinch of salt
3 tablespoons butter
1 tablespoon shortening
4 or 5 tablespoons water
1 10-ounce package frozen chopped spinach
5 tablespoons sour cream
1 large egg
1 teaspoon grated nutmeg
Salt and pepper to taste

Sift flour and salt into a bowl. Cut in butter and shortening with 2 knives or a pastry blender until mixture resembles cornmeal. Add the water to make a firm pastry dough. Chill 1 hour before rolling out. Use 6 to 8 glass custard cups for tart pans. Line with pastry, and flute edges.

Cook spinach according to package directions. Drain and purée in a blender. Combine sour cream, egg, and spinach. Season to taste with nutmeg, salt, and pepper. Spoon into pastry and cook 3 cups at a time on "defrost" or coolest setting for 12 minutes or until knife inserted near center comes out clean. Test every 2 minutes during end of cooking period. Tarts will not brown without special unit.

green peas bonne femme

Frozen peas could be substituted for fresh peas in this recipe. Cooking time would be 12 minutes for a 20-ounce package of frozen peas.

Yield: 6 servings

¼ pound bacon, cut in 1-inch pieces	½ cup water
2 tablespoons butter	½ teaspoon salt
3 cups fresh green peas	¼ teaspoon pepper
6 small white onions	1 tablespoon sugar
Inner leaves of a lettuce	1 tablespoon finely chopped parsley

Fry bacon in a 1-quart glass casserole on the highest setting for 3 minutes. Add butter, peas, onions, lettuce, water, salt, and pepper. Cover and cook on highest setting for 10 minutes. Add sugar after 8 minutes. When peas are done, drain remaining liquid. Sprinkle with parsley before serving.

fresh peas in the french manner

For this recipe, the peas are cooked in very little water. They are kept moist with the addition of shredded lettuce leaves.

Yield: 4 servings

2 pounds peas in the pod
8 small whole white onions, peeled, with a cross cut in the root end
6 Boston lettuce leaves or 1 Bibb lettuce, shredded
1 teaspoon sugar
½ teaspoon salt
3 tablespoons butter
3 tablespoons water
1 tablespoon cornstarch dissolved
   in 1 tablespoon cold water

Shell the peas and place in a 1½-quart glass or ceramic casserole with all the remaining ingredients except the cornstarch. Cover and cook on the highest setting for 8 minutes. Stir in the cornstarch dissolved in cold water and stir gently taking care not to break the peas. Cook for 1 minute. Serve hot.

green beans with parmesan cheese

Buy crisp, young, fresh green beans for this recipe.

Yield: 4 servings

1½ pounds string beans	2 tablespoons butter
¼ cup water	2 tablespoons finely chopped parsley
1 teaspoon salt	Freshly ground black pepper
¼ cup freshly grated Parmesan cheese	

Trim and wash the beans. Place in a shallow 10-inch glass dish and add water and salt. Cover with waxed paper and cook for 8 minutes on the highest setting. Drain and rinse immediately under cold running water. Return to the dish and sprinkle with cheese. Dot with butter. Cook uncovered for 2 minutes. Sprinkle with finely chopped parsley and season with pepper.

green peas bonne femme

braised endives

Braised endives are an extraordinarily fine accompaniment for fish and simple roast meats.

Yield: 2 servings

4 Belgian endives	2 tablespoons grated Swiss cheese
1 tablespoon butter	1 tablespoon grated Parmesan cheese
1 teaspoon Dijon mustard	Salt and pepper
½ cup heavy cream	1 tablespoon finely chopped parsley

Cut a V shape in the base of each endive to remove the bitter core. Remove the blemished outer leaves. Arrange the endives in a 9-inch glass or ceramic baking dish. Add the butter, mustard, cream, and cheeses. Cover with waxed paper and cook on the highest setting for 4 minutes. Season with salt and pepper and garnish with parsley.

pepper salad

This is an Italian inspiration. The green pepper strips form a crunchy contrast of texture with the soft succulence of the tomatoes. Serve the salad with cold chicken or other cold meat.

Yield: 6 servings

2 medium-size green peppers	½ teaspoon basil
3 large summer-ripe tomatoes, sliced	2 tablespoons red wine vinegar
3 scallions, finely chopped	6 tablespoons olive oil
½ teaspoon salt	3 tablespoons chopped chives
Freshly ground black pepper	

Cut the green peppers into strips and cover with boiling water. Cook on the highest setting for 2 minutes. Drain and rinse immediately under cold running water.

Arrange the green pepper strips and tomato slices in a serving dish and sprinkle with scallions. Combine all the remaining ingredients and pour over the salad.

braised celery

If desired serve with extra butter.

Yield: 4 servings

1 bunch celery	1 chicken bouillon cube, dissolved
½ teaspoon salt	in 1 cup boiling water
¼ teaspoon pepper	1 tablespoon finely chopped parsley
2 tablespoons butter	

Cut off green leaves from celery and discard. Cut celery stalks in half. Wash well and place in a glass casserole. Season with salt and pepper. Dot with butter and pour chicken stock over celery.

Cover dish and cook on highest setting for 10 to 12 minutes. Sprinkle with finely chopped parsley.

corn and tomato casserole

Another summer dish—to be served when the corn is local and gathered the same day it is cooked.

Yield: 6 servings

4 medium-size tomatoes
3 tablespoons butter
1 onion, finely chopped
2 stalks celery, finely chopped
1 green pepper, finely chopped
3 tablespoons flour
1½ cups milk

3 egg yolks
½ cup grated Parmesan cheese
Salt and pepper
3 hard-boiled eggs, sliced
8 ears corn, approximately
    2 cups corn

Peel, seed, and chop 3 of the tomatoes. Slice the remaining tomato. Heat the butter on the highest setting for 40 seconds and add the onion, celery, and green pepper. Cook 2 minutes. Stir once. Stir in the flour and cook 30 seconds. Stir in the milk with a wire whisk. Season with salt and pepper. Cook 3 minutes, until the sauce has thickened. Stir in the egg yolks combined with the Parmesan cheese. Arrange the chopped tomato, sliced eggs, and corn in a 10-inch baking dish. Cover with the sauce. Cover with waxed paper and cook on "simmer" setting for 8 minutes. Stir once after 2 minutes to be sure the center of the custard will be completely cooked. Let stand 2 minutes. Top with slices of tomato.

potatoes stuffed with shrimp

With a tossed salad these potatoes can become a whole meal.

Yield: 4 servings

4 large baking potatoes
2 tablespoons butter
2 egg yolks
2 tablespoons whipping cream
Salt and pepper
Dash Tabasco sauce

1½ cups cooked small shrimps
2 tablespoons chopped chives
1 cup grated cheddar cheese
2 tablespoons chopped
    chives or parsley
Parsley for garnish

Pierce the potatoes with a fork or skewer in two places. Arrange the potatoes 1 inch apart on paper plates and cook for 12 minutes on the highest setting. Turn the potatoes over after 6 minutes and rotate the dish one-quarter of a turn. Leave the potatoes to stand for 5 minutes.

Cut a slice from the top of each potato and use a teaspoon to scoop out the inside. Take great care not to break the potato shells. Place the potato centers in a mixer and add the butter, egg yolks, and cream. Mix until smooth mashed potatoes are formed. Season with salt, pepper, and Tabasco sauce. Stir in the shrimps, chives, and half of the grated cheese. Place the mixture in the potato shells and sprinkle with the remaining cheese. Return the potatoes to the microwave oven and cook for 3 minutes on the highest setting. Rotate the potatoes one-quarter of a turn and cook for 2 more minutes.

pineapple syrup pudding

desserts

pineapple syrup pudding

This steamed pudding can be cooked very successfully in a microwave oven.

Yield: 6 servings

1 pound 14 ounce can pineapple slices	¾ cup light brown sugar
2 tablespoons butter	3 large eggs
2 tablespoons corn syrup	3 cups self-rising flour
5 maraschino cherries	1 tablespoon baking powder
¾ cup vegetable shortening	

Drain pineapple rings; reserve juice. Spread butter inside a 2-quart glass bowl. Spread syrup over the butter. Place 1 pineapple ring in bottom of bowl and arrange 4 rings around the sides. Put a cherry in the center of each pineapple ring.

Chop the remaining pineapple rings. Place shortening, brown sugar, eggs, and pineapple in a mixing bowl. Sift flour and baking powder into the bowl. Beat mixture for several minutes. Add enough pineapple juice to give a soft consistency. Spoon into prepared bowl. Cover with glass lid or plastic wrap. Cook on "simmer" setting for 12 minutes. Cook on highest setting for 2 or 3 minutes or until a toothpick comes out clean. Remove lid; let stand 5 minutes, unmold. Serve hot or cold.

pineapple gateau

This is a delicious dessert for any occasion.

Yield: 6 servings

3 large eggs	2 teaspoons baking powder
¾ cup sugar	16-ounce can pineapple rings
1 tablespoon cold water	1¼ cups heavy cream
¾ cup flour	3 tablespoon red currant jelly
¾ cup cornstarch	

Beat eggs, sugar, and water for 15 minutes or until very thick and creamy. Sift flour with cornstarch and baking powder. Fold into beaten egg mixture; lightly and carefully. Line the bottom of a 9-inch round baking dish with waxed paper. Pour mixture into the prepared dish. Cook on "simmer" setting for 7 minutes. Continue cooking on high for 3 or 4 minutes or until a toothpick comes out clean. Let cake stand 5 minutes to set. Turn out on serving plate to cool.

Drain the pineapple and chop finely. Whip cream and butter. Put half of cream in a pastry bag fitted with a medium star nozzle. Put the red currant jelly in a bag fitted with a fine plain nozzle. Cut cake in half. Spread half the remaining cream on 1 piece of cake. Spoon pineapple on top. Place other piece of cake on top and spoon remaining cream on top. Pipe on shell border of jelly around the top edge of cake. Pipe lines of red currant jelly in the center.

caramel custard

This smooth custard is surrounded with a caramel sauce.

Yield: 6 servings

¼ cup granulated sugar
3 eggs
2 egg yolks
⅓ cup sugar
2 cups milk
1 teaspoon vanilla extract

Place the sugar in a 1-quart glass or ceramic casserole. Cook in the microwave oven for 5 minutes on the highest setting. Swirl the sugar around the casserole after 2 minutes so that it will melt evenly to form a caramel. The bowl will become hot, so use oven mitts. Rotate the casserole to coat the bottom and sides evenly with caramel.

Stir together the eggs, egg yolks, and sugar until just combined. Heat the milk in a 4-cup glass measuring cup for 2 minutes on the highest setting. Stir the hot milk into the eggs and sugar. Add the vanilla and pour into the caramel-lined casserole. Cook uncovered on "simmer" setting for 8 minutes. Stir the custard and rotate the dish one-quarter of a turn every 2 minutes. Cool.

Chill the custard for 4 hours and invert on a serving plate with a small rim. The caramel will form a sauce around the custard.

chocolate pudding

An excellent after-school snack for the children.

Yield: 6 servings

6 ounces sweet chocolate
½ cup sugar
2 tablespoons cornstarch
3 cups milk
3 eggs, lightly beaten
1 teaspoon vanilla

Break the chocolate into squares and put on a plate. Cook in the microwave oven on the highest setting for 2 minutes.

Measure the sugar, cornstarch, and milk into a 1-quart glass or ceramic bowl and cook for 2 minutes. Stir in the melted chocolate and the lightly beaten eggs with a wire whisk and cook on "roast" setting for 4 minutes. Add the vanilla. Stir and chill for 4 hours before serving.

orange curls
(Garnish for Chocolate Pudding)

With a sharp knife or potato peeler, peel orange thinly, taking care to keep skin in one piece. Put a star of whipped cream in the center of the pudding by filling a waxed-paper cone with whipped cream.

molded rice pudding with chocolate sauce

A creamy rich dessert that makes a fine ending to a meal. The chocolate sauce is also good on ice cream.

Yield: 6 servings

1 cup long-grain rice	1 teaspoon vanilla extract
2 cups cold water	2 packages unflavored gelatin
1½ cups milk	2 tablespoons cold water
½ cup sugar	1 cup heavy cream, whipped
4 egg yolks	

Place the rice in a 1-quart glass casserole. Cover with cold water. Cover and cook for 10 minutes on the highest setting. Let stand for 10 minutes. Drain off any excess water. In the meantime, pour the milk into a 4-cup glass measuring cup. Add the sugar and cook for 1½ minutes. Stir in the egg yolks and vanilla extract. In a custard cup sprinkle the gelatin on the surface of the water. Cook in the microwave oven for 10 seconds, until the gelatin has dissolved.

Combine the rice, custard, gelatin, and whipped cream. Place in a 1½-quart oiled mold. Chill for 4 hours and unmold.

chocolate sauce

1 package (6 ounces) semisweet chocolate pieces	2 tablespoons butter
¼ cup water	1 cup heavy cream
	1 teaspoon vanilla extract

Place all the ingredients in a 4-cup glass measuring cup. Cook 1 minute on the highest setting. Stir and cook 1 minute longer on "simmer" setting. Stir rapidly with a wire whisk to form a smooth sauce.

orange curls

oranges in syrup

A light dessert that's special any time of the year.

Yield: 6 servings

6 large, perfect eating oranges
1 cup sugar
1 cup water
2 tablespoons Grand Marnier

Peel the colored part of the orange rind very thinly, with a potato peeler. Cut the peel into strips the length of a matchstick and half the width. Remove all the white pith and cut each orange in half through the center, horizontally. Reassemble the oranges with toothpicks.

To prepare the syrup, put the sugar, water, and julienne strips of orange peel in a 2-quart glass bowl. Cook for 5 minutes on the highest setting. Add the Grand Marnier. Place the oranges in the hot syrup and allow to cool. Chill 4 hours before serving.

baked apples

One baked apple can be made in the microwave oven in 2 minutes. A word of warning: If you decide to top the apple with raspberry preserves or maple syrup it will be excruciatingly hot in this time. Eat it carefully!

Yield: 4 servings

4 crisp Rome Beauty or other baking apples
4 teaspoons raisins
½ cup water
4 tablespoons chopped pecans or other nuts
1 teaspoon cinnamon
½ cup pure maple syrup or fruit preserves

Remove ¾ of the apple peel, leaving only a supporting ring around the base. Remove the core and put the apple to one side.

Place the raisins in a 1-cup glass measuring cup with the water and cook on the highest setting for 1 minute. Drain the raisins.

Fill the apples with raisins and nuts. Dust with cinnamon and cover with maple syrup or preserves. Cover with waxed paper and cook for 8 minutes.

french fruit tarts

Attractive tart shells can be cooked on inverted custard cups. Favorite pastry or pie crust mixes could be substituted for the following rich pastry.

Yield: 10 to 12 shells

¼ cup butter
¼ cup sugar
2 egg yolks
1 cup flour
Apricot jam
2 or 3 varieties of fruit—cherries, nectarines, mandarin oranges, grapes,
**   peaches, pineapple, strawberries, plums**

Combine butter, sugar, and egg yolks and work together with fingers until smooth. Work in flour and knead to form a smooth dough. Form into a ball and put into a plastic bag. Chill for 30 minutes before rolling and cutting to fit inverted glass custard cups. Chill again for 1 hour before baking. Prick pastry before cooking. Bake on "reheat" setting for 1½ minutes for 4 tarts. If a brown crust is desired, transfer to a preheated 450°F conventional oven and cook a few minutes.

The tart shells may be made a week in advance and stored in the refrigerator. Heat for 1 or 2 minutes on "reheat" setting to crisp the crust before filling. Brush the inside of shells with strained warm jam, arrange the fresh or well-drained canned fruit in the shells, and brush with jam.

pear pie with red wine

pear pie with red wine

This is a unique dessert for a special occasion.

Yield: 6 servings

8- or 9-inch pie crust, frozen or homemade

filling

6 large, fresh Anjou pears
⅓ cup sugar
2 teaspoons cinnamon
1 cup red wine

Line an 8- or 9-inch glass pie plate with pie crust. Flute edge; prick bottom and sides of crust with fork. Cook on "roast" setting for 7 minutes. Meanwhile cut pears in half, peel and remove cores. In a glass bowl, add pears, sugar, cinnamon, and wine. Cover bowl with a plate and cook on highest setting for 6 minutes. Fill the pie crust with the fruit and pour wine over pears. Cook on highest setting for 6 to 8 minutes or until pears are tender. Serve warm.

poached pears in wine syrup

Fruits poached in the microwave oven retain their color and texture very well. This is an excellent dessert, quickly made. Serve it alone, with whipped cream, English custard sauce, or ice cream.

Yield: 4 servings

1 cup sugar
2 cups red wine
¼ teaspoon allspice
1 teaspoon candied ginger, chopped
1 cinnamon stick
4 Anjou pears, cut in half, core removed but peel left on

Place the sugar, wine, allspice, ginger, and cinnamon stick in a 10-inch round glass baking dish. Bring to the boiling point on the highest setting. It will take approximately 4 minutes. Cook on "simmer" setting for 10 minutes. Arrange the pears in the dish and cook on the highest setting for 5 minutes. Leave the pears to cool in the syrup. Chill for 4 hours before serving.

lemon meringue pie

Though pastry does not brown in the microwave oven, it will become crisp and flaky and taste very good. The meringue topping is completed in the conventional oven.

Yield: 8 servings

	lemon filling	meringue
1¼ cups flour	⅔ cup cornstarch	4 egg whites
¼ teaspoon salt	1¼ cups sugar	⅛ teaspoon cream of
3 tablespoons shortening	2 cups water	tartar
3 tablespoons butter,	4 egg yolks	¼ teaspoon salt
cut into small pieces	Grated rind and juice	1 cup sugar
¼ cup water	of 2 lemons	

Place the flour, salt, and shortening in a bowl and blend with a pastry blender until the pieces are the size of small peas. Blend in the butter and stir in the water with a fork. Form the dough into a ball and roll on a floured board. Fit into a 9-inch pie plate. Prick the bottom and sides of the pastry with a fork. Cook on the highest setting for 8 minutes. Rotate the pie plate one-quarter of a turn after 4 minutes.

To prepare the filling, measure the cornstarch, sugar, and water into a 4-cup measuring cup. Cook for 2 minutes on the highest setting. Stir in the egg yolks and the grated rind and juice of the lemons. Spread the filling in an even layer in the baked pastry shell. Cook on "roast" setting for 4 minutes.

To prepare the meringue, preheat the oven to 250°F. Place the egg whites, cream of tartar, and salt in the mixer and beat until soft peaks are formed. Add the sugar gradually and beat until stiff and shiny. Spread the meringue on top of the lemon filling and cook in the conventional oven for 40 minutes, until the meringue is lightly browned.

Note: The meringue cannot be cooked in the microwave oven even in the models that have a browning unit. The meringue will completely disintegrate in the microwave oven.

rhubarb cream

A light, fresh-tasting dessert with the consistency of a mousse.

Yield: 8 servings

1½ pounds rhubarb
1 cup sugar
½ cup water
2 envelopes gelatin, dissolved in ⅓ cup cold water
1 cup heavy cream, whipped

Cut the rhubarb into 1-inch pieces and place in a 1½-quart glass or ceramic casserole with the sugar and ½ cup of the water. Cover and cook on the highest setting for 7 minutes. Stir once so the rhubarb cooks evenly. Purée the rhubarb with the liquid in the blender and allow to cool.

Sprinkle the gelatin over the water in a custard cup and let stand for 3 minutes. Heat in the microwave oven for 1 minute, until the gelatin has dissolved. Fold the gelatin and whipped cream into the purée. Transfer to a serving dish and chill in the refrigerator for 4 hours, until set.

french apple flan

This is a delicious light dessert for any occasion.

Yield: 6 servings

¼ cup butter	1 cup flour
½ cup sugar	4 large cooking apples
2 large egg yolks	3 tablespoons apricot jam, strained
½ teaspoon vanilla extract or essence	

Combine butter, ¼ cup sugar, and egg yolks and work together with fingers until smooth. Add vanilla extract and mix well. Work in flour and knead to form a smooth dough. Form into a ball and put into a plastic bag. Chill for 30 minutes and roll out to fit an 8- or 9-inch glass pie plate. Prick bottom and sides of crust with fork. Cook on "roast" setting for 6 minutes.

Meanwhile, wash, peel, core, and thinly slice cooking apples. Place one-third of the apple slices in the pastry shell; sprinkle on 2 tablespoons of remaining sugar. Repeat. Arrange the remaining apples in an attractive ring on top. Cook on high for 7 minutes or until apples are soft. Remove from oven.

Heat apricot jam in a small custard cup on highest setting for 1 minute. Brush jam over flan while hot.

apple brown betty

The microwave is a constant delight. The more you use it the more uses can be found for it. This traditional American dessert is a marvelous combination of soft, spicy apples and crisp bread crumbs. Serve it with whipped cream, ice cream, or English custard sauce.

Yield: 6 servings

3 cups bread crumbs made from Italian or French bread
¾ cup sugar
⅛ teaspoon freshly grated nutmeg
1 teaspoon cinnamon
½ cup butter
4 medium-size cooking apples, peeled, cored, and very thinly sliced
½ cup raisins
½ cup water

Form the bread into crumbs in the blender. Heat the microwave ceramic plate for 4 minutes on the highest setting. Add 2 tablespoons of the butter and cook for 30 seconds, until melted. Spread half the crumbs in an even layer on the plate. Cook for 1 minute. Stir. Cook for 1 minute more, until the crumbs are lightly browned and crisp. Repeat with the remaining crumbs. Stir together the crumbs, sugar, and spices.

Butter a 2-quart soufflé dish or similar bowl. Place a layer of ⅓ of the crumbs in the bowl.

Place the raisins in a 1-cup glass measuring cup and cover with ½ cup water. Cook in the microwave oven for 1 minute and drain.

Top the layer of bread crumbs with a layer of half the apples and raisins. Add a layer of crumbs, then the remaining apples and raisins. Finish with a top layer of crumbs. Dot with the remaining butter and cook on "roast" setting for 10 minutes.

hot fudge sauce

Add ¼ cup of dark rum to this sauce if you are serving it with poached or canned pears. It is very rich and smooth.

Yield: 1½ cups

2 squares unsweetened baking chocolate
½ cup water
2 tablespoons butter
¼ cup white corn syrup
1 cup sugar
6 ounces semisweet chocolate pieces
¼ cup heavy cream

Place the baking chocolate on a plate and cook in the microwave oven on the highest setting for 1 minute.

Transfer the melted chocolate to a 4-cup glass measuring cup and add the water, butter, corn syrup, and sugar. Cook on the highest setting for 2 minutes. Stir in the semisweet chocolate and cream. The semisweet chocolate will melt in the heat of the sauce.

butterscotch sauce

Be very careful with this sauce because the sugar becomes extremely hot very quickly, and it may boil over if you take your eye off it. Do not taste it immediately or it will burn your mouth.

Yield: 1 cup (enough ice cream topping for 6 servings)

1 cup brown sugar
3 tablespoons butter
½ cup heavy cream
1 teaspoon vanilla

Measure the sugar, butter, and cream into a 4-cup glass measuring cup. Cook on the highest setting for 1 minute, then on "roast" setting for 30 seconds and "defrost" setting for 20 seconds. Stir, and add vanilla.

english custard sauce

Here is a sauce to serve with Apple Brown Betty or poached fruit.

Yield: 2 cups

1¾ cups milk
¼ cup sugar
3 egg yolks
1 tablespoon cornstarch

Pour 1½ cups of the milk into a 4-cup glass measuring cup. Add the sugar and cook in the microwave oven on the highest setting for 2 minutes.

Stir together the egg yolks, cornstarch, and remaining ¼ cup of cold milk. Add the hot milk and sugar. Cook on the highest setting for 1 minute. Stir briskly with a wire whisk.

Cookie dough may be made 4 or 5 days in advance and kept in a plastic bag in the refrigerator. Leave the dough at room temperature for 1 or 2 hours before making the cookies.

Yield: 16 cookies

¾ cup shelled hazelnuts or walnuts   **1¼ cups flour**
½ cup butter   **¼ teaspoon salt**
¼ cup brown sugar

Set 16 nuts aside. Place remaining nuts on a baking tray and cook in a conventional oven, 350°F, until the skins loosen and the inner nut is turning golden. Rub in a towel to remove skins. Then grind nuts in a grater or coffee grinder.

Beat butter in a bowl and beat in the sugar. Add the nuts, sifted flour, and salt. Roll into 16 balls and pat out with a wet fork in 2 flat-bottomed greased baking dishes. Set a nut in the center of each. Cook 1 dish at a time on "simmer" setting for about 5 minutes. Cool before removing from dish. Dust with confectioner's sugar. Brown for a minute under a conventional broiler.

chocolate and orange cake

chocolate and orange cake

This elegant cake is delicious, too!

Yield: 6 servings

1 cup butter	1 small banana
1 cup sugar	1 pineapple ring (from can)
4 eggs, beaten	¼ cup chocolate frosting
1 orange	½ cup confectioner's sugar
2 cups self-rising flour	Yellow food coloring
¾ cup whipping cream	

Line the bottoms of 2 round glass baking dishes with waxed paper. Beat butter and sugar together. Add eggs, one at a time, beating well, and grated orange rind. Reserve rest of orange. Sift flour and fold into mixture. Spoon into baking dishes and bake one at a time. Cook on "simmer" setting for 7 minutes. Continue cooking on highest setting for 3 to 4 minutes or until toothpick inserted near center comes out clean. Repeat for second layer. Let cake stand 5 minutes before turning out on serving plate.

Whip cream, sweetened to taste, and mix in sliced banana. Section orange and reserve 3 sections. Chop rest and fold into cream. Cut pineapple into pieces. Reserve 3 pieces of pineapple and fold remainder into cream. Spread over 1 layer.

Cut other cake into 6 wedges. Frost 3 wedges with chocolate icing. Top with pineapple.

Sift confectioner's sugar; add just enough water to make smooth icing. Add food coloring to color pale yellow and spread on 3 wedges. Decorate with orange. Assemble cake as shown. Refrigerate and serve within a few hours.

chocolate and molasses cake

Line the bottoms of glass baking dishes with waxed paper. This method is more successful than greasing and flouring cake dishes.

Yield: 6 to 8 servings

1 tablespoon cocoa powder, regular, not instant	1½ cups flour
¼ cup butter	2 teaspoons baking soda
¼ cup sugar	2 tablespoons molasses
1 large egg	⅓ cup warm milk
	Optional decoration: candied cherries

Blend cocoa powder with 3 tablespoons hot water and let cool. Beat butter with sugar until light and fluffy. Gradually add the egg, beating well. Mix in cocoa and butter.

Sift flour with baking soda. Mix molasses with warm milk. Fold flour and molasses alternately into the creamed mixture.

Line the bottom of a 9-inch round glass baking dish with waxed paper. Pour mixture into prepared dish. Cook on "simmer" setting for 7 minutes and then on highest setting for 3 to 4 minutes or until a toothpick inserted in the center comes out clean. Cool for 5 minutes before removing from dish.

Decorate with halves of candied cherries.

chocolate and molasses cake

brownies

These rich chocolate morsels are cooked in 4½ minutes.

Yield: 16 squares

4 squares (1 ounce each)
  unsweetened chocolate
6 tablespoons butter
2 eggs
1 cup sugar

1 cup sifted all-purpose flour
½ teaspoon salt
½ teaspoon baking powder
1 teaspoon vanilla extract
½ cup chopped walnuts or pecans

Line an 8 x 8-inch glass baking dish with buttered waxed paper. Break the chocolate into small pieces and place in a bowl with the butter. Cook in the microwave oven on the highest setting for 1 minute 30 seconds, until the chocolate has completely melted. Beat the eggs and sugar together until creamy. Sift the flour with the salt and baking powder. Stir all the ingredients together. Spread the mixture evenly into the baking dish. Cook for 4½ minutes, rotating the dish one-quarter of a turn twice during the cooking period. Cool the brownies in the dish. Remove the paper and cut the brownies into squares.

chocolate frosted brownies

Yield: 16 squares   1 recipe brownies

icing

3 tablespoons butter
¼ cup cocoa, sifted

3 tablespoons evaporated milk
1 cup confectioner's sugar, sifted

Melt butter with cocoa in small glass bowl on highest setting for 30 seconds. Stir and cook for 1 minute. Remove from heat and add evaporated milk, then stir in confectioner's sugar. Spread over brownies and let set.

banana-nut bread

Quick breads baked in the microwave oven tend to become soft on the bottom unless they are baked in a dish lined with waxed paper. This excellent bread is cooked in 8 minutes. Spread with butter, it makes a delicious snack with a glass of milk. It is also good with southern fried chicken.

Yield: 16 squares
½ cup butter
¾ cup brown sugar
1 ripe banana, mashed
1 teaspoon lemon juice
2 eggs

1¼ cups flour
½ teaspoon baking powder
½ teaspoon baking soda
½ teaspoon salt
¼ teaspoon nutmeg
½ cup chopped pecans

Cream the butter and sugar together. Mix the banana, lemon juice, and eggs. Sift together the flour, baking powder, baking soda, salt, nutmeg, and pecans. Combine the 2 mixtures, stirring until the flour is just combined.

Bake in an 8-inch square glass or ceramic baking dish lined with waxed paper for 8 minutes on the highest setting. Turn the dish one-quarter of a turn every 2 minutes. Leave the bread in the pan for 5 minutes. Transfer to a cooling rack, waxed paper side down, and leave to cool for 10 minutes. Peel off the paper and cut into 16 squares.

victoria lemon cake

A Victoria Cake will keep moist for days if kept in an airtight container or plastic bag.

Yield: 10 to 12 slices

1 cup sweet butter
Grated rind of ½ lemon
1 cup sugar
4 eggs
2 cups self-rising flour
1 to 1½ cups lemon pudding
¼ cup confectioner's sugar

Cream butter until soft. Add lemon rind. Gradually beat in sugar until the mixture is soft and pale. Beat eggs lightly and stir into the mixture a little at a time. Sift flour onto mixture and fold in with a spatula.

Line the bottoms of 2 round medium-size glass baking dishes with waxed paper. Divide mixture equally between the dishes. Cook one at a time on "simmer" setting for 7 minutes and then on highest setting for 3 to 4 minutes or until a toothpick comes out clean. Let cake stand 5 minutes to set. Spread lemon pudding on top of one layer and place second layer on top. Sprinkle with confectioner's sugar.

banana cake

Here is a chance to use your artistic flair.

Yield: 8 to 10 servings

1 cup butter
1 cup sugar
4 large eggs, beaten
4 medium-size ripe bananas
3 small lemons
3 cups self-rising flour, sifted
2 tablespoons cornstarch
¼ cup sugar
Yellow food coloring
1 cup heavy cream,
  whipped and sweetened
¼ cup milk
Optional extra: candy lemon slices

Line the base of 2 round glass baking dishes with waxed paper. Beat the butter with 1 cup sugar until light and fluffy. Gradually add the eggs, beating well.

Mash 2 bananas and beat into the mixture. Grate the rind from 2 lemons and add to the mixture. Fold in sifted flour. Spoon into prepared dishes. Bake one layer at a time. Cook on "simmer" setting for 7 minutes. Continue cooking on highest setting for 3 to 4 minutes or until toothpick inserted near center comes out clean. Repeat for second layer. Let cake stand for 5 minutes before turning out on serving plate.

Squeeze juice from lemons. Reserve 2 tablespoons. Add enough water to lemon juice to make 1¼ cups. Stir cornstarch into lemon juice and water in a small glass bowl. Add ¼ cup sugar and a few drops of food coloring. On highest setting, bring to boil and cook for 2 minutes. Stir once after 1 minute. Cover with lid or plastic wrap and cool.

Place ⅓ whipped cream in a decorating bag fitted with a star nozzle. Pipe 12 circles around the edges of one of the cakes (as shown in picture).

Beat the lemon mixture and place a little in the center of each circle. Peel and slice the remaining bananas and brush with reserved tablespoon of lemon juice. Arrange half of bananas in a circle on top of the cake. Place lemon candy in center. Spread the remaining lemon mixture, whipped cream, topping, and bananas between the layers. Serve within 2 hours.

banana cake

index